Beautiful
Monterey Peninsula
and Big Sur

"Learn about America in a beautiful way."

Beautiful
Monterey Peninsula
and Big Sur

Concept and Design: Robert D. Shangle
Text: Brian Berger

First Printing November, 1980
Published by Beautiful America Publishing Company
P.O. Box 608, Beaverton, Oregon 97075
Robert D. Shangle, Publisher

Library of Congress Cataloging in Publication Data
Beautiful Monterey Peninsula
1. Monterey Peninsula, Calif.—Description and travel—Views. I. Title.
F868.M7B47   979.4'76   80-20374
ISBN 0-89802-164-2
ISBN 0-89802-163-4 (paperback)

Copyright © 1980 by Beautiful America Publishing Company
Printed in the United States of America

Photo Credits

JAMES BLANK—*page 18; page 22; page 34; page 37; page 38; page 39; page 49; page 60.*

JOHN HILL—*page 17; page 20; page 31; page 52; page 58.*

PHILIP MILLER—*pages 56-57.*

ROBERT SHANGLE—*page 27; page 62; page 63.*

STEVE TERRILL—*page 19; page 21; page 23; pages 24-25; page 26; page 28; page 29; page 30; page 32; page 33; page 35; page 36; pages 40-41; page 42; page 43; page 44; page 45; page 46; page 47; page 48; page 50; page 51; page 53; page 54; page 55; page 59; page 61; page 64.*

**Color Separations
by
Universal Color Corporation
Beaverton, Oregon/San Diego, California**

Contents

Introduction..7

The Setting 9

Settlement 12

Exploring the Peninsula 15

The Peninsula in Literature 66

MONTEREY PENINSULA

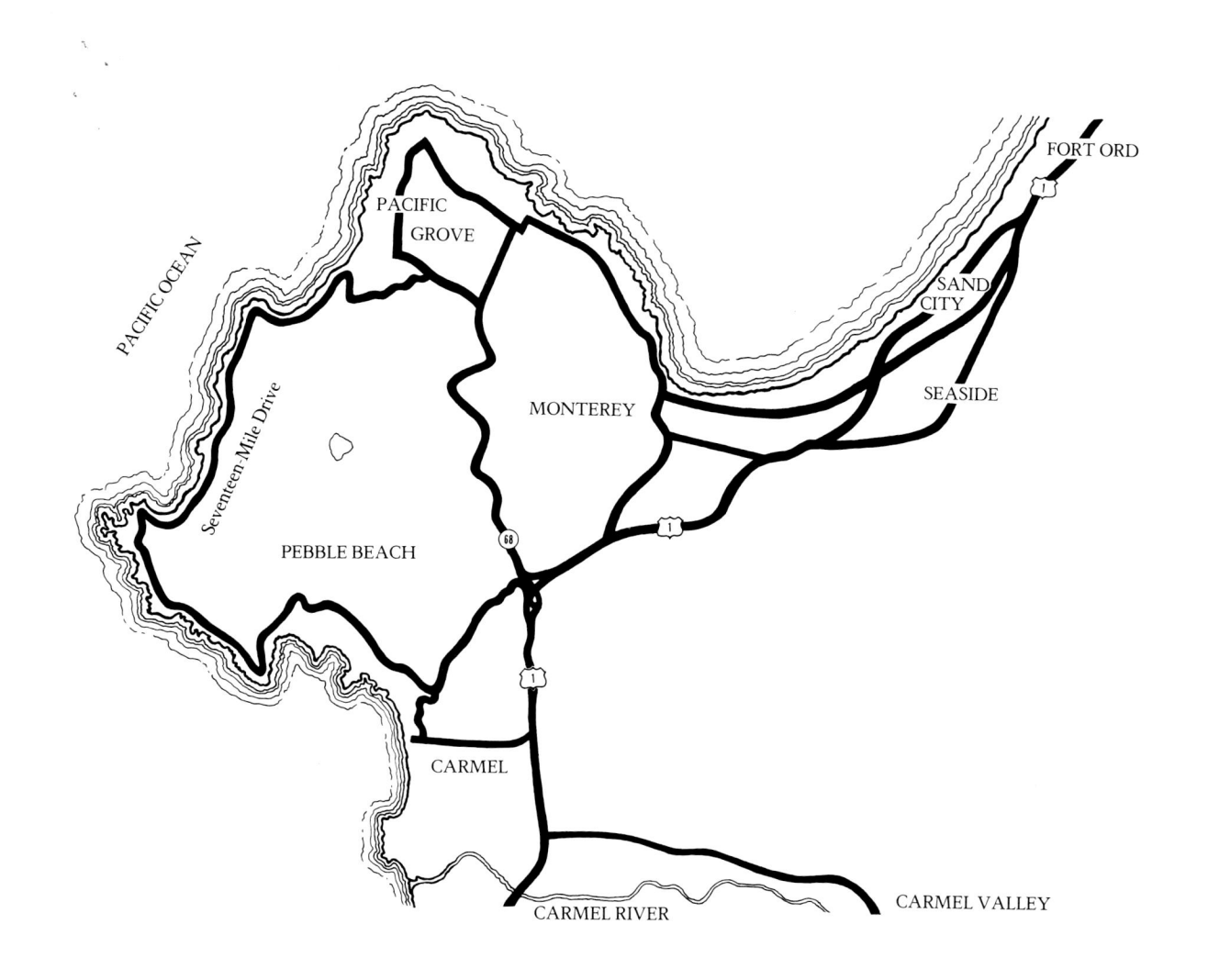

Introduction

"...here is the final unridiculous peace. Before the first man
Here were the stones, the ocean, the cypresses,
And the pallid region in the stone-rough dome of fog where the
   moon
Falls on the west. Here is reality."

Robinson Jeffers, *Hooded Night*

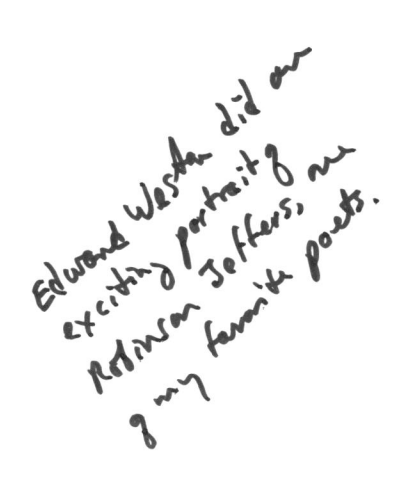

For Robinson Jeffers, whose verse rhythms resembled the "movement of waves, the pulse of blood, the cadences of speech," the Monterey Peninsula and its environs proved the perfect inspiration. Here the blanched trunks of windswept Monterey cypress trees seem a twisted, gnarled extension of the granite rock masses to which they cling. Tufts of greenery sprout from branches, seemingly long dead and withered, the leaves drawing nourishment from the trees' persistent inner vitality. Looking like ancient parchment scrolls, the thin, brick-red bark of the madrone tree peels in the midday sun, revealing the lighter skin beneath.

Gulls, soaring, dipping flashes of gray and white, skim Monterey Bay's waters, flapping wildly in the wake of a trawler loaded with rockfish. Tidepools harbor a jewel-like collection of seashore life. Grouped in tight bunches, like some exotic flowering plant, goose-neck barnacles and blue-tinted mussels cling to wave-swept rocks—awaiting the incoming tide and its microscopic life. Sunset paints the western slopes of the Santa Lucia Mountains with a soft, orange glow. Night sees hundreds of herring gulls abandon their noisy, daytime search for food, settling on rocky outcroppings like miniature sentinels, waiting for the first signs of dawn. From out of the vast blackness of a moonless night, a misty tide sweeps inland from the ocean, covering a sleeping peninsula and filling the valley of the Carmel River.

Except for the carefully controlled intrusions of man, this was the scene that greeted the merchant-explorer Sebastian Vizcaino, who, in 1602, was sent to explore the coast of California for the Count of Monte-Rey, Viceroy of Mexico. Some have said that Vizcaino was overly exuberant when reporting to the Viceroy that Monterey Bay was "the best port that could be desired . . . sheltered from all winds, it has many pines for masts and yards, and live oaks and white oaks, and water in great quantity, all near the shore." Perhaps the bay was not the most eligible California port for the Viceroy's galleons, but none can fault Vizcaino for his praise of this land; he merely succumbed to its manifold beauties.

Today the Monterey Peninsula fits the description of the "Riviera of the Americas." Within the Peninsula's 25 square miles of rugged beauty are the guarded houses of the very rich, many hidden in the forested area of Seventeen Mile Drive. And at Carmel-by-the-Sea, artists and writers have gathered near the fresh, salty air of the Pacific Ocean, inspired by the magnificence of the surroundings.

In the town of Monterey, old adobe structures have been preserved and carefully restored, reminders of Old Monterey's Spanish and Mexican heritage. Cannery Row, edging Monterey Bay, appears outwardly unchanged from when the writer, John Steinbeck, used it as a setting for his novel of the same name. But it is only the facade that remains; the fish canneries, saloons, and hotels that made Cannery Row famous between the years 1920 and 1945 have long since disappeared—vanished—like the sardines on which the canneries once depended. Cannery Row now houses unique gift shops, art galleries, and restaurants.

At Fisherman's Wharf, the smell of cooked squid, spiced with wine, garlic, and parsley, overpowers the salty, coastal air. Displays of freshly boiled crab lure passersby to taste their tender, brine-flavored meat. Anchored in neat rows out in the bay, tall-masted sailboats form colorful patterns on the undulating waters.

A golfer's paradise, the Peninsula's 17 golf links are known for their unique landscape. The 16th hole of the Cypress Point Golf Course, which is part of the heavily wooded Del Monte Forest, lies on the rocky shoreline. Elsewhere, the famed Pebble Beach fairways play host to the Bing Crosby National Pro-Amateur golf tournament every January, the course known for its spectacular scenery as well as for its toughness.

Historically attractive, recreationally challenging, intellectually exciting, the Monterey Peninsula has much to offer to the visitor. But for those who have chosen to live here, they enjoy the very essence of this land—a quality that the writer Robert Louis Stevenson best captured when long ago he wrote of the Peninsula:

> The one common note of all this country is the haunting presence of the ocean. A great faint sound of breakers follows you high up into the inland canyons. . . . The woods and the Pacific rule between them the climate of the seaboard region. . . . When the air does not smell salt from the one it will be blowing perfume from the resinous tree tops of the other.

Brian Berger

The Setting

Between the bays of Monterey and Carmel, a rugged thumb of land pushes five miles into the Pacific's wind-tossed waters. Where this headland meets the full fury of the ocean, the land lies gnawed and twisted. Great pieces of the Peninsula's rocky shoreline have been pulverized by eons of wave action, and finely ground particles have been deposited to form the promontories' glistening white beaches.

Among the Peninsula's rocks, tidepools harbor small communities of colorful marine life. Occasionally, a vacant abalone shell flashes its rainbow colors amid the embattled rocks. High on the Peninsula's craggy cliffs, other evidence of the land's battle against the elements can be seen in the twisted, windblown shapes of the Monterey cypress. Bent from the attack of countless storms, the trees cling to their granite perches with an age-tested perseverance. Farther inland, the cypress gradually give way to the almost equally adhering Monterey pine—tall, with deeply ridged trunks. East of the Peninsula, madrone and redwood climb into the coastal hills.

Offshore, the rugged bulk of Seal Rock is astir with the heavy bodies of countless sea lions. Great masses of quivering ungainliness, the males test their loud barkings against the Pacific's deeper roar. Nearby, Bird Rock is alive with preening sea gulls and cormorants, the latter looking like animated, black bowling pins. Closer to shore, the occasional sea otter can be seen floating on its back, giving the appearance of a contented tourist enjoying the surf.

Among the pines in the community of Pacific Grove, bright clusters of goldenbrown Monarch butterflies gather in October. Driven to warmer climes by the approach of winter in western Canada, the Monarchs make their annual pilgrimage to the Peninsula to mate and lay their eggs on the milkweed plants of the area. Sometimes forming groups of nearly a thousand on a single branch, their spreading wings appear as bunches of sun-washed, autumn leaves. Disturbed by a gust of wind, the Monarchs disappear in a fluttering, golden swarm.

Just south of the Monterey Peninsula, the steep-walled Point Lobos State Reserve juts into the Pacific's ever-restless waters. Here, as on the Peninsula, the cypress aline themselves like withered sentinels along the outer portions of the rugged headland. Winding trails cut through springtime meadows spotted with buttercups, lupine, and poppies. Elsewhere, thick stands of pine hide an abundance of animal life.

Backdropping the coastline southeast of Point Lobos, the Santa Lucia Range parallels State Highway 1 for more than 100 miles. A barrier against coastal storms, the Lucia's 800- to 5,000-foot ridges slope into narrow canyons and valleys, where ponderosa, sugar pines, oak, and laurel grow, surrounded by an endless blanket of scrub. Sometimes during the summer months, the ocean cannot be seen from even the highest of the Santa Lucia ridges. Instead, a thick, rolling layer of fog spreads inland, filling the canyons of this coastal range and weaving a misty path far up the Carmel Valley. At these times the Monterey Peninsula lies hidden under a mantle of pearl-gray luminance, the rugged edges of its cliffs softened by the opaque mist.

Where the northern portions of the Santa Lucias plunge into the Pacific, ending in steep, wave-battered cliffs, lies the magnificent Big Sur Country. Here, nearly undisturbed by the presence of man, is the primal meeting of continent and ocean. Winter breakers chisel the rocky cliff faces with an infinite patience, sculpting sea caves and irregular arches. Swirling vapor, from the waves' explosive contact with the land, rises from between the headlands like steam. Dusk will turn the sea to a red wine color, and the ravines of the Santa Lucias reflect purple hues.

On the eastern slopes of the Santa Lucias spread the fertile Salinas and Carmel valleys. Here the rich browns of newly plowed earth contrast with green fields of strawberries, broccoli, and lettuce. Spring paints the surrounding hills with the pastel shades of lupine and brighter patches of sun-yellow poppies. At Castroville, near the Salinas Valley's western end, thousands of acres of artichoke plants display their plump, green buds.

East of the Salinas Valley stand the low, dry Gabilan Mountains. Digger pine flourishes here, among a carpeting of yellow grasses. Burned by the heat of a relentless summer sun, the upper slopes of the Gabilans exhibit a rich, golden tint. Farther down the slopes, cattle graze in the noonday heat, which tries to draw the last traces of precious moisture from the arid land. Night will bring its welcomed coolness to these parched hills, prompting predators—coyote, fox, and bobcats—to begin their search for food.

North of the Peninsula, the shoreline sweeps in a great arc toward the town of Santa Cruz, forming the Bay of Monterey. Beneath the Bay waters lurk a rich harvest of marine life. Hidden in a rocky recess near the shore, a retiring octopus may survey the depths with bulging yellow eyes, awaiting an unwary crab that might venture within the reach of its snake-like tentacles. Clinging to a nearby rock with its broad, muscular foot, abalone feed on a patch of algae, a hard, protective shell blending with the surroundings. Brightly colored crab dance stiff-legged across the sandy bottom, seeking the camouflaging cover of seaweed beds. Equally colorful—but slower moving—starfish seem to glide along the bay's floor on their tube-endowed appendages, hoping to dine on a tasty clam.

Above the Bay's waters, the winds from far out to sea are skipping over incoming swells, helping to keep the temperature of the region a moderate 56 to 67 degrees Fahrenheit throughout the year. These same winds bring the comforting blankets of fog that sometimes lie above the Peninsula for days, shielding it from the oppressive heat that bakes the inland regions during the summer months. Robert Louis Stevenson wrote:

> The upper air is still bright with sunlight, but the fogs are in possession of the lower levels; they crawl in scarves among the sandhills . . . where they have struck the seaward shoulder of the mountains of the Santa Lucia, they double back and spire up skyward like smoke. Where their shadow touches, color dies out of the world . . . . It takes but a little while till the invasion is complete. The sea, in its lighter order, has submerged the earth.

Settlement

It was the Portuguese captain, Juan Rodriquez Cabrillo, who on November 17, 1542, was the first European to sail into the sparkling waters of Monterey Bay. Under orders from the King of Spain to explore the coast of California for the legendary "Strait of Anian" (the Northwest Passage), Cabrillo, although delighted by the unexpected discovery of Monterey Bay, decided to continue his mission rather than go ashore. But before weighing anchor, Cabrillo claimed the bay and the lands surrounding it for "God and Phillip II," naming what is now the Monterey Peninsula *Punta de los Pinos*, or Point of Pines.

It was 60 years later before another European, Sebastian Vizcaino, entered this "noble harbor," naming it for his patron, the Count of Monte-Rey, Viceroy of Mexico. Unlike Cabrillo, Vizcaino quickly organized a landing party to explore this new land. He reported that the "climate and the quality of the soil [resembled] Castile," with a large port "sheltered from all winds [and providing] protection and security for the ships coming from the Philippines." By the time Vizcaino had run out of superlatives, his description of the Monterey country compared favorably with that of the Garden of Eden.

Unfortunately for Vizcaino, his hopes of commanding the next expedition to Monterey would not be realized. A new Viceroy was installed soon after he had returned with his glowing report, and this successor to the Count of Monte-Rey looked unfavorably toward any further explorations of the California coast. But Vizcaino's report would be published, and over a century-and-a-half later it would be used to guide a third Spanish expedition to Upper California, but this time it would be overland from Mexico.

The Spanish had been uneasy about rumors of British and Russian interest in Alta (Upper) California, and so in 1769 they sent Don Gaspar de Portola to establish a garrison at Monterey. So grand had been Vizcaino's description of Monterey Bay, that Portola was unable to recognize it for what it was, even after identifying the Point of Pines and the Carmel River. Instead he continued on to San Francisco, before realizing he must have missed the harbor. On his return trip south to San Diego, Portola definitely identified what he termed "Vizcaino's hallucination," and planted two crosses on a hill overlooking the bay. A year later Portola returned with settlers and soldiers, and established a *presidio* (garrison) and a mission, San Carlos Borromeo. Monterey was now officially the capital of Alta California.

Over the next half century, the Spaniards continued to build California. The Indians were utilized as a source of cheap labor, allowing the owners of large ranchos to lead a life of aristocratic idleness. But while the Spaniards indulged in the good life, they failed to note the growing bitterness of the Mexican people to Spanish rule. By the time they took the matter seriously, Mexico had already launched a full-scale revolution, forcing Spain to grant her independence in 1822. Monterey was now a Mexican possession.

Mexico was to have even less luck at holding onto California than did Spain. Political intrigue blinded the Mexican people to the growing American presence in California—settlers who had crossed the continent in what was the vanguard of the westward movement. The Americans were even more land hungry than the Mexicans, believing that it was their manifest destiny to own all of the land along the shores of California—even if it meant robbing the Mexican landowners of their territory. Fearing that the French or British might beat him to it, President James Polk sent American military forces to secure California, and on July 7, 1846, the American flag was raised over the Custom House at Monterey.

After the American occupation, Monterey began to grow rapidly. Distrustful of the native adobe, the new residents sent for lumber to be shipped around Cape Horn. With bricks and chalkrock as additional building material, carpenters introduced New England touches to the prevailing architectural styles: a beautifully preserved example is Colton Hall, built in 1847-49.

No sooner had the population of Monterey begun to increase when the discovery of gold, at a sawmill on the American River, quickly depopulated it. So struck with gold fever were some of the town's residents, that a few left unfinished bottles of liquor tottering on tables, while the owner of a recently opened boarding house rushed out of town before her lodgers could pay their bills. The only ones left in Monterey were women, prisoners, and a few soldiers.

Almost on the heels of this blow to Monterey's hopes of a large population came the word that California's capital was being moved to San Jose. Monterey became almost a ghost town. Its growth over the next 25 years would come nearly to a standstill, a period of time remembered as a romantic isolation. Whaling was the town's only industry of importance during these years, but its main support came from the large ranchos in the area.

By 1875 Monterey was beginning to show signs of awakening once again. The Southern Pacific Railroad had lines through the Salinas Valley, bringing new settlers to the area. Agriculture was taking the place of cattle raising, as the large ranchos were divided into acreage for the planting of wheat and other crops. A small colony of Chinese fishermen was capitalizing on the bountiful supply of fish off of Monterey's coastline, exporting more than 100 tons of dried fish annually. The natural beauty of the region was gradually discovered by tourists, prompting the building of "The Christian Seaside Resort," later to become Pacific Grove.

Monterey's reputation as a restful, scenic wonder continued to grow, and by the first years of the 20th century, artists and writers began to form a settlement on the Peninsula's south side—known then as The Village. Here, overlooking the waters of Carmel Bay, gathered a small pocket of the literary elite: writers and poets such as George Sterling, Mary Austin, Sinclair Lewis, William Rose Benet, and Upton Sinclair. Robinson Jeffers was drawn here in 1914, two years before The Village was incorporated as "Carmel-by-the-Sea." He became the Peninsula's most famous literary figure.

At the same time that Carmel-by-the-Sea was incorporated, silver was discovered in the Peninsula's coastal waters. But this *silver* needed no pick-and-shovel to claim it, only the finely meshed nets used by fishermen from boats. Seemingly inexhaustible supplies of silvery sardines led to the rapid construction of nine canneries along Monterey's shoreline, and in a short time the town was being billed as the "sardine capital of the world."

The sardine supply did not last. The fishermen gathered all that their nets could hold, until the source was depleted. In the 1940s John Steinbeck wrote: "The pearl-gray canneries of corrugated iron were silent and a pacing watchman was their only life. The street that once roared with trucks was quiet and empty."

Today the Peninsula is a tourist's delight. The canneries that once clanged with the noise of packing machines now ring with the sound of cash registers, collecting the dollars spent at Cannery Row's fine restaurants, shops, and galleries. The Peninsula's stunning scenery, recreational opportunities, and historical significance give the visitor an untiring enthusiasm for the area.

Exploring the Peninsula

Finished in 1845, and later enlarged to accommodate Monterey's growing commerce, Fisherman's Wharf is a browser's and seafood gourmet's delight. Serenaded by the occasional barking of sea lions looking for a handout and the hungry cries of gulls, visitors to the Wharf can pass the better part of an afternoon just strolling through the pier's many art and gift shops. When the aroma of baked shrimp and crab or sauteed scallops becomes irresistible, the visitor will find that any of the Wharf's excellent restaurants can satisfy the most discriminating taste. Before leaving the Wharf, the true aficionado will want to stop at one of the fish markets to pick up the necessary ingredients for some private gourmet cooking.

Just across the *Presidio* from Fisherman's Wharf stands the one-time center of Monterey's sardine-canning industry—Cannery Row. This was once a noisy gathering of 30 fish canneries, calling their crews to work with blasts from distinctively toned whistles. The Row is now a pathway of epicurian treats and smart shops. Here, as on Fisherman's Wharf, one can spend a full day searching for some unique gift made by a local artist, or just relaxing with a steaming plate of the native cuisine.

A walking tour of historic Old Monterey is a must if one is to savor the full flavor of the town's Spanish beginnings. Here are preserved examples of Monterey's unique architectural heritage; many of the buildings now serve as museums, private homes, offices, and civic clubs. Known to be the largest collection of restored adobes in the United States, these buildings owe their preservation to the efforts of the town's concerned citizens.

The "Path of History," a three-mile route marked with red arrows, will lead the visitor past 45 of these historical structures—one of which was once occupied by the famed novelist Robert Louis Stevenson, and another by John C. Fremont, then a Major in the California Battalion. Many of the buildings are furnished much as they were in the 18th and 19th centuries, causing one to reflect about the daily living conditions of the town's early residents.

Monterey County is known as a wine producing region, with many of its vineyards lining U.S. Highway 101, between the towns of San Lucas and Chualar. It is for this reason that the Peninsula has been chosen as the site for the annual California Wine Festival, first held here in December of 1976. Gathering at the beautiful Monterey Conference Center, hundreds of amateur and professional oenologists (students of wines), from all parts of the nation, attend seminars given by a number of well-known wine authorities. Four days are spent tasting the products of many California wineries, all participants leaving a little happier than when they first arrived.

Another annual Monterey event is the eagerly awaited Monterey Jazz Festival. Held in mid-September, it began in 1957. For three days the Monterey County Fairgrounds are alive with the sounds of such artists as John Lewis, Clark Terry, Connie Kay, Mundell Lowe, Slide Hampton, Richie Cole, and Bob Brookmeyer. Among some of the well-known groups that keep things humming, one can expect the New Dave Brubeck Quartet, the Cal Tjader Sextet, and Manhattan Transfer.

Between New Monterey and Point Pinos spreads the picturesque community of Pacific Grove. Established in 1875 as "The Christian Seaside Resort," and known in later years as "Pacific Grove Retreat," the town's early boosters claimed its climate was "the most equable in the known world, and with a location so healthy that doctors scarcely make a living." Today Pacific Grove is best known as "Butterfly Town, U.S.A.," because of the thousands of Monarch butterflies that take up residence here annually. The town's residents are so fond of these migrant insects, they have passed a city ordinance that prescribes a fine of $500, or six months imprisonment, or both, for anyone caught harming them.

Besides the enjoyment one can find in browsing through Pacific Grove's many gift and antique shops, there is the special attraction of the town's beach playground, a sheltered spot of warm, white sands and picnic areas. After a refreshing swim, visitors can drive along Ocean View Boulevard and stop to tour the Point Pinos Lighthouse, whose first lamp used whale oil and was visible for some 16 miles.

Much of the Monterey Peninsula's most dramatic scenery can be viewed while traveling its celebrated Seventeen Mile Drive. Begun in the 1880s and completed in 1916, this "Circle of Enchantment" skirts some of the Peninsula's finest examples of Monterey cypress. It encompasses the mansions of many famous people; parallels a shoreline of magnificent vistas; and passes the finely manicured fairways of famed golf courses. Connecting as it does, Monterey, Pacific Grove, and Carmel-by-the-Sea, a trip around the Drive is an enjoyable way to absorb the ambience of the Peninsula.

Carmel-by-the-Sea, located on the Peninsula's southern shoreline, has gained the reputation of being a haven for artists and writers. It was here in the early 1900s that

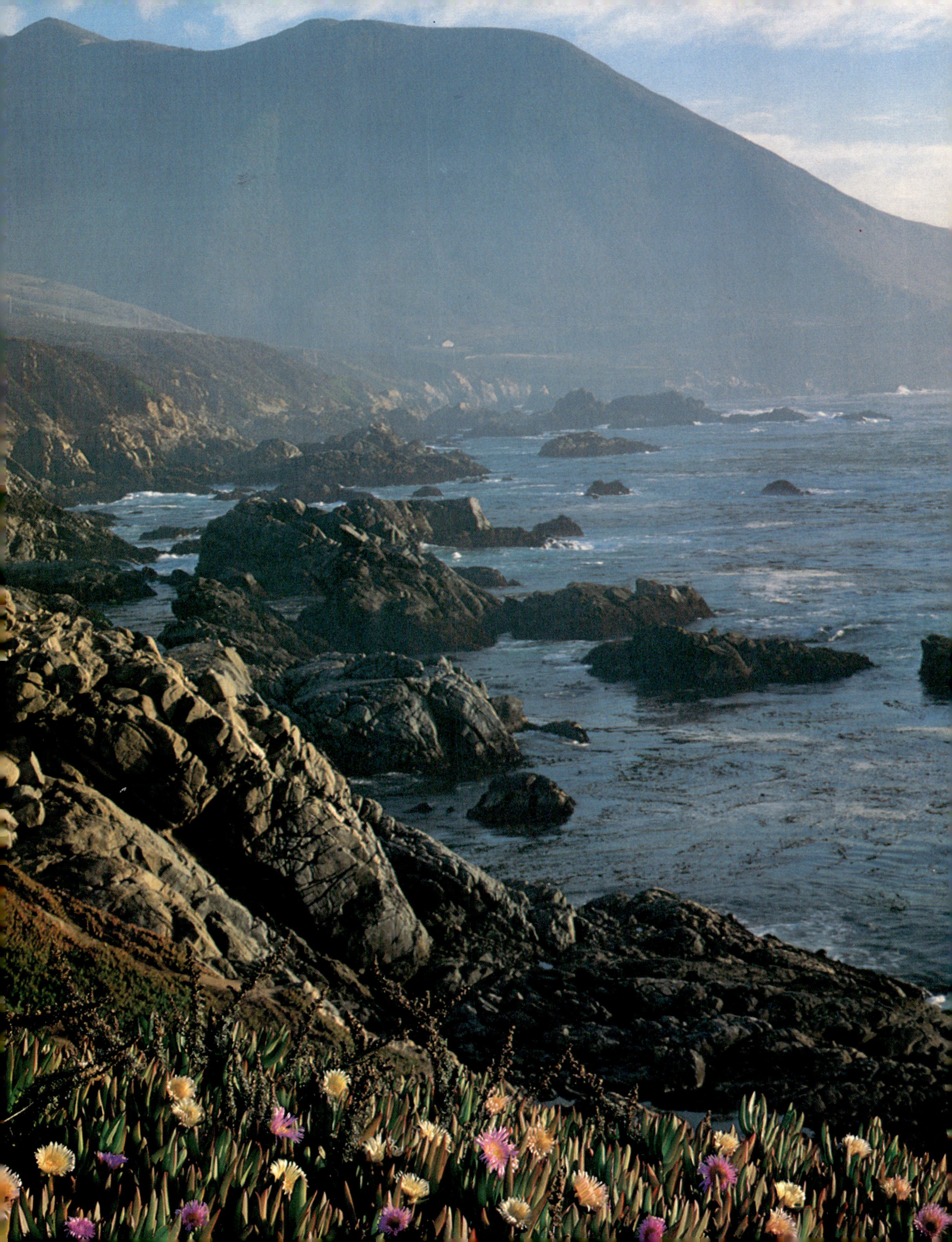

The Marina at Monterey

Carmel Mission

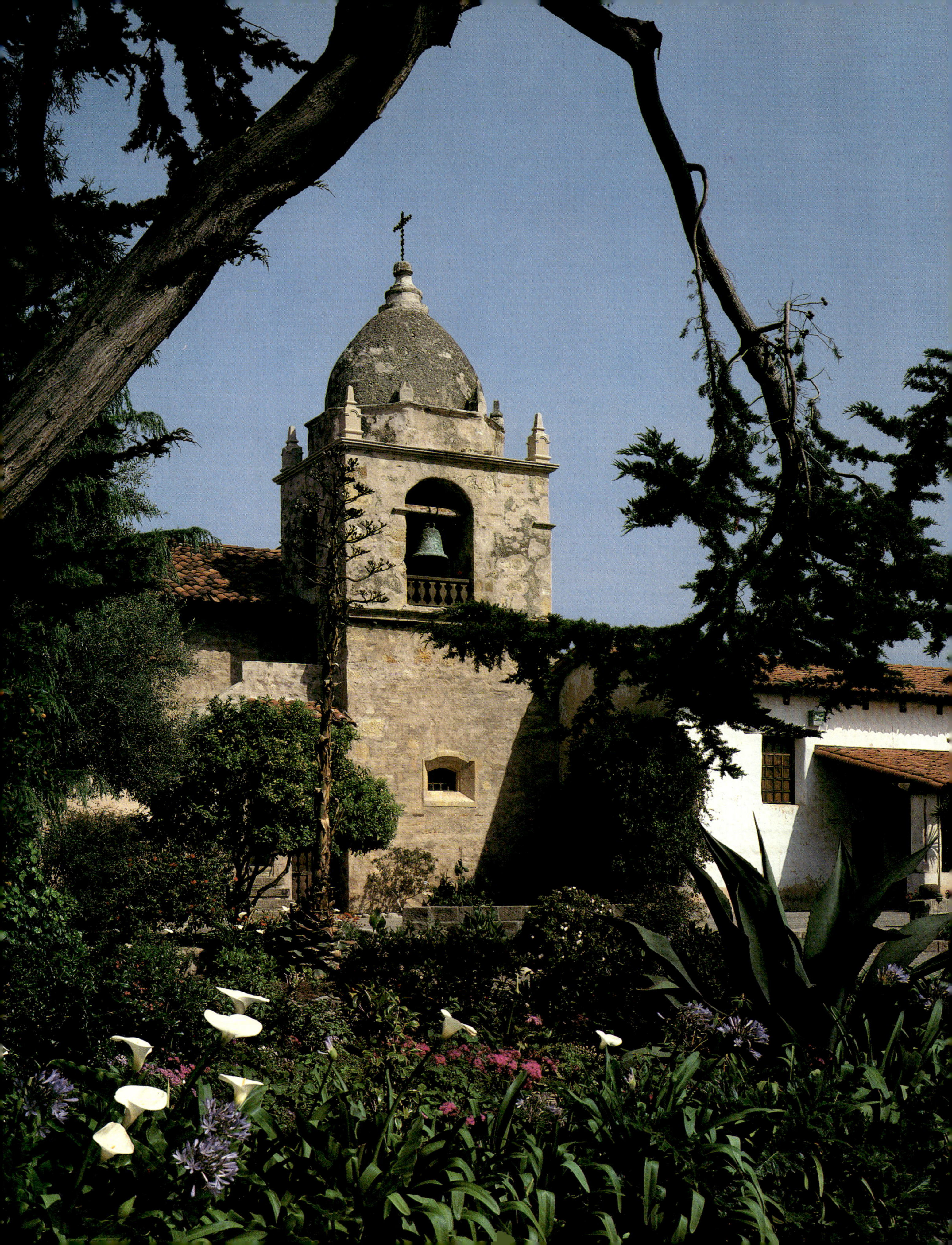

The coastline south of Big Sur

Poppies along the Big Sur Highway

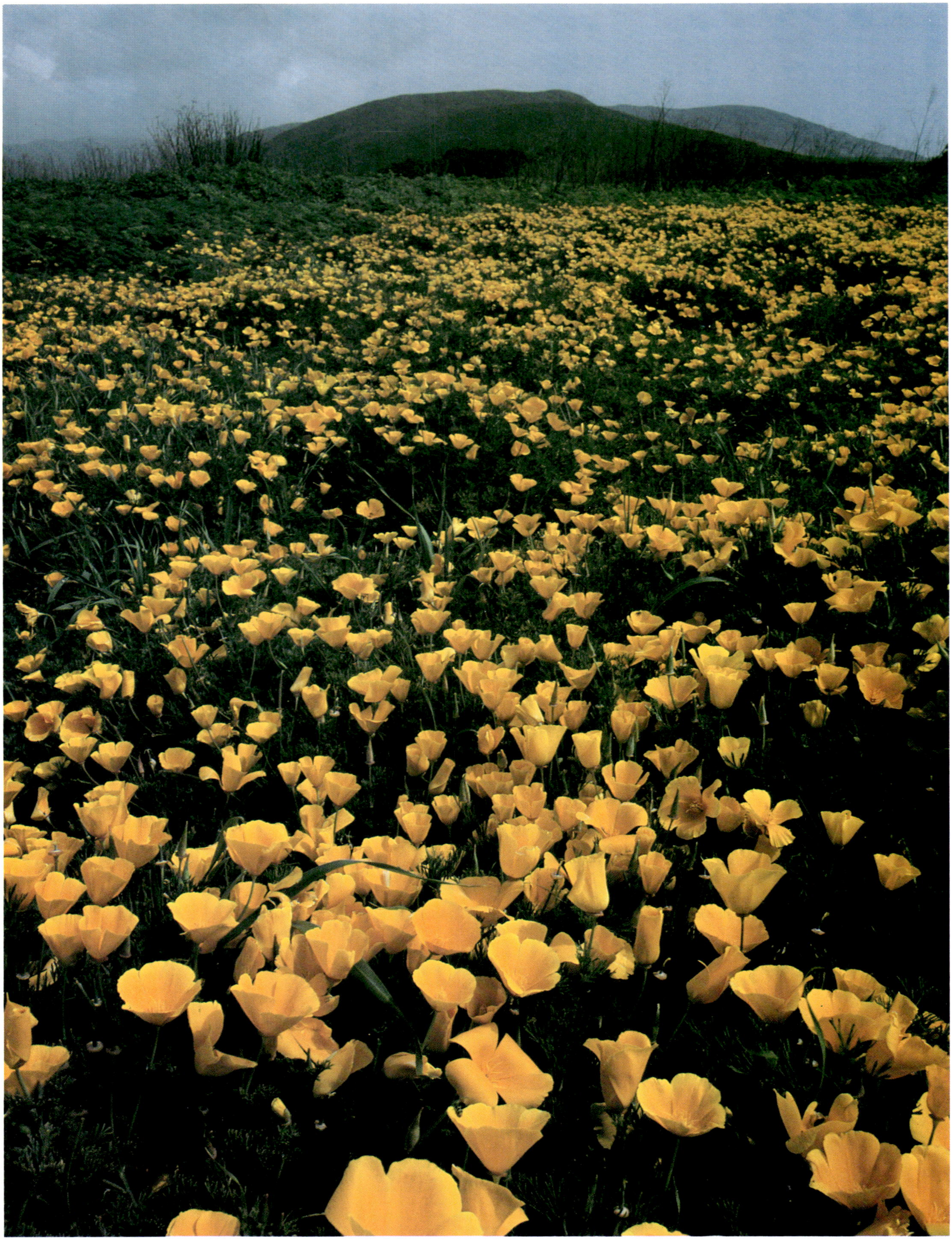

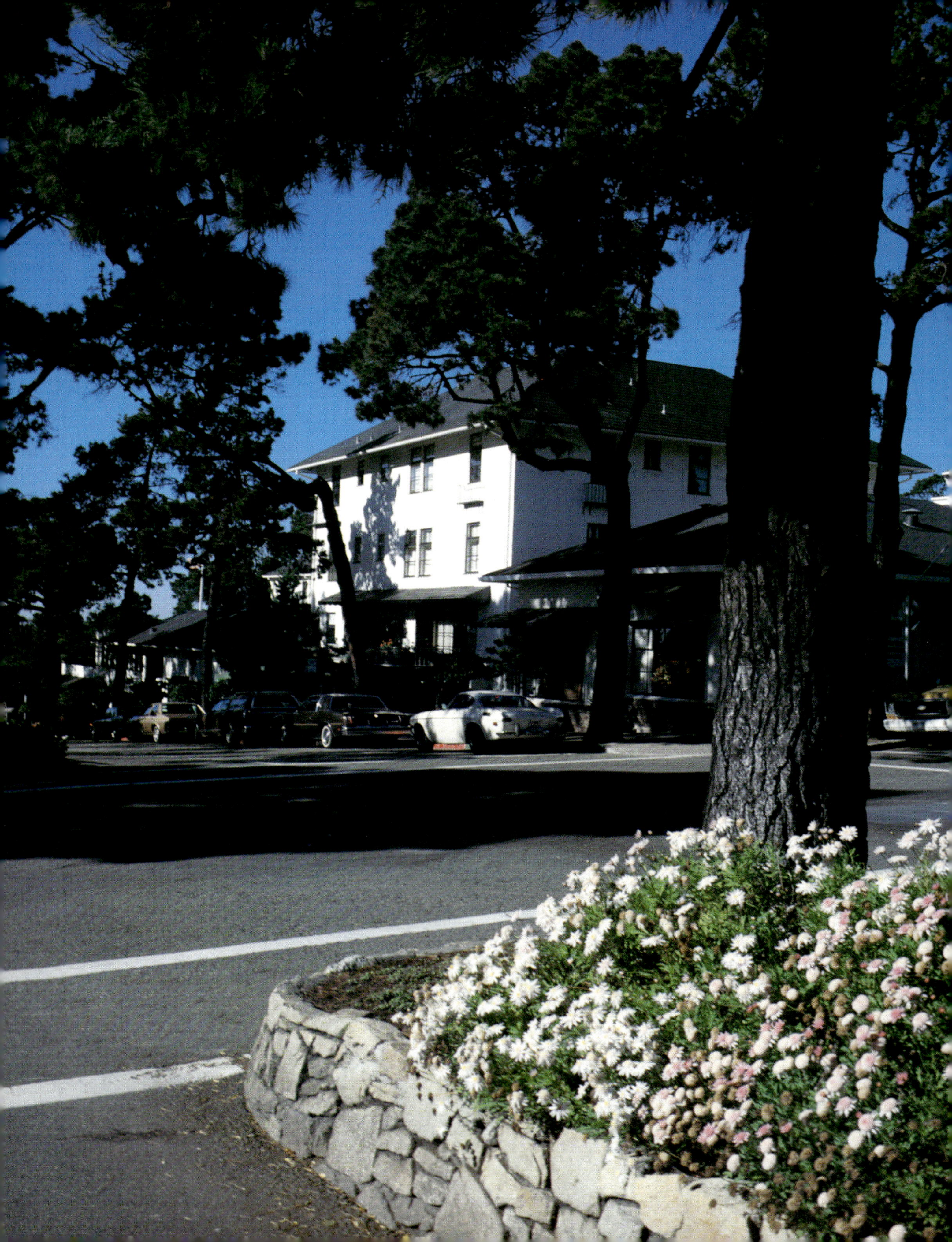

Black egret, Pacific Grove
(Following pages) Sunrise at Santa Cruz

Ocean Avenue in downtown Carmel

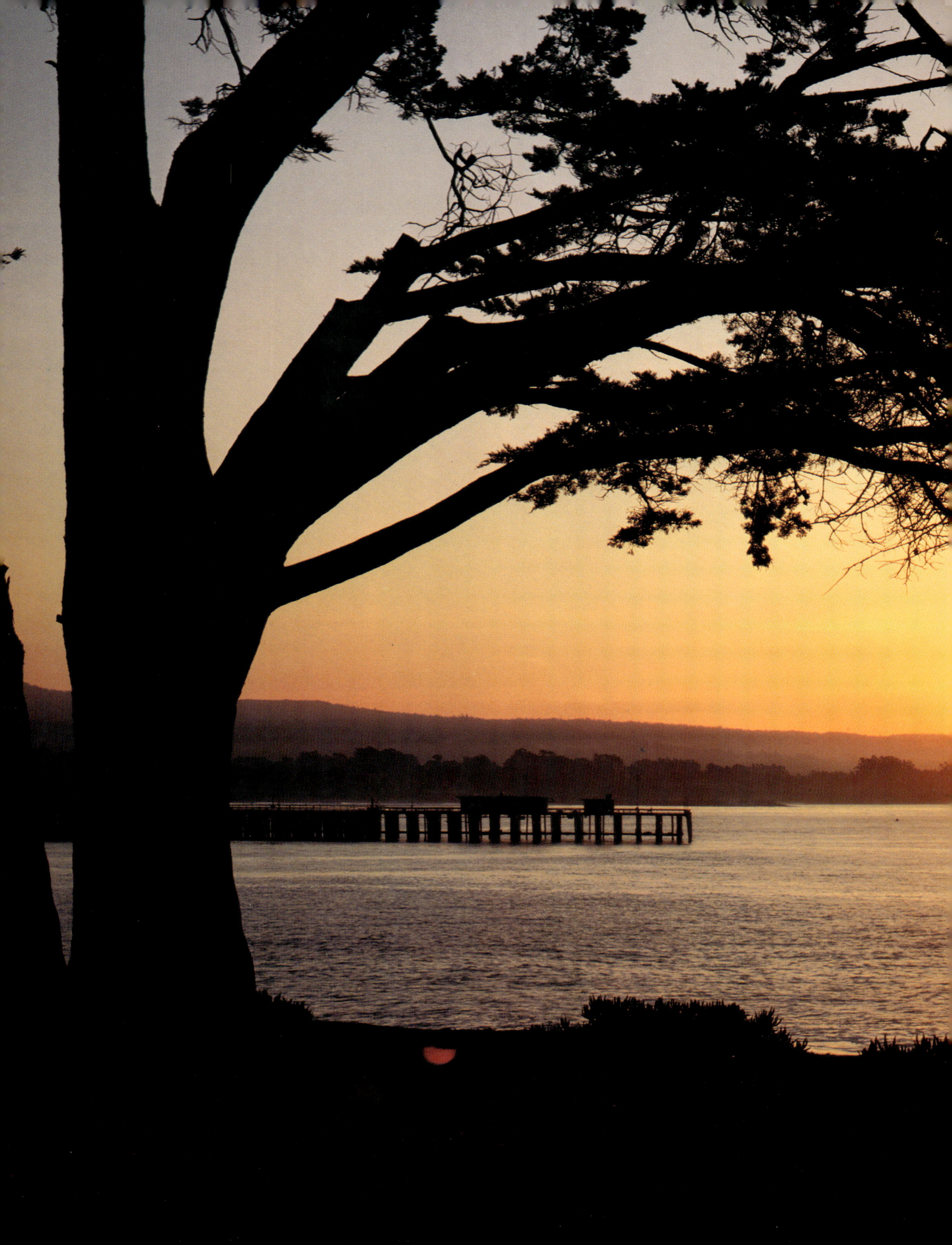

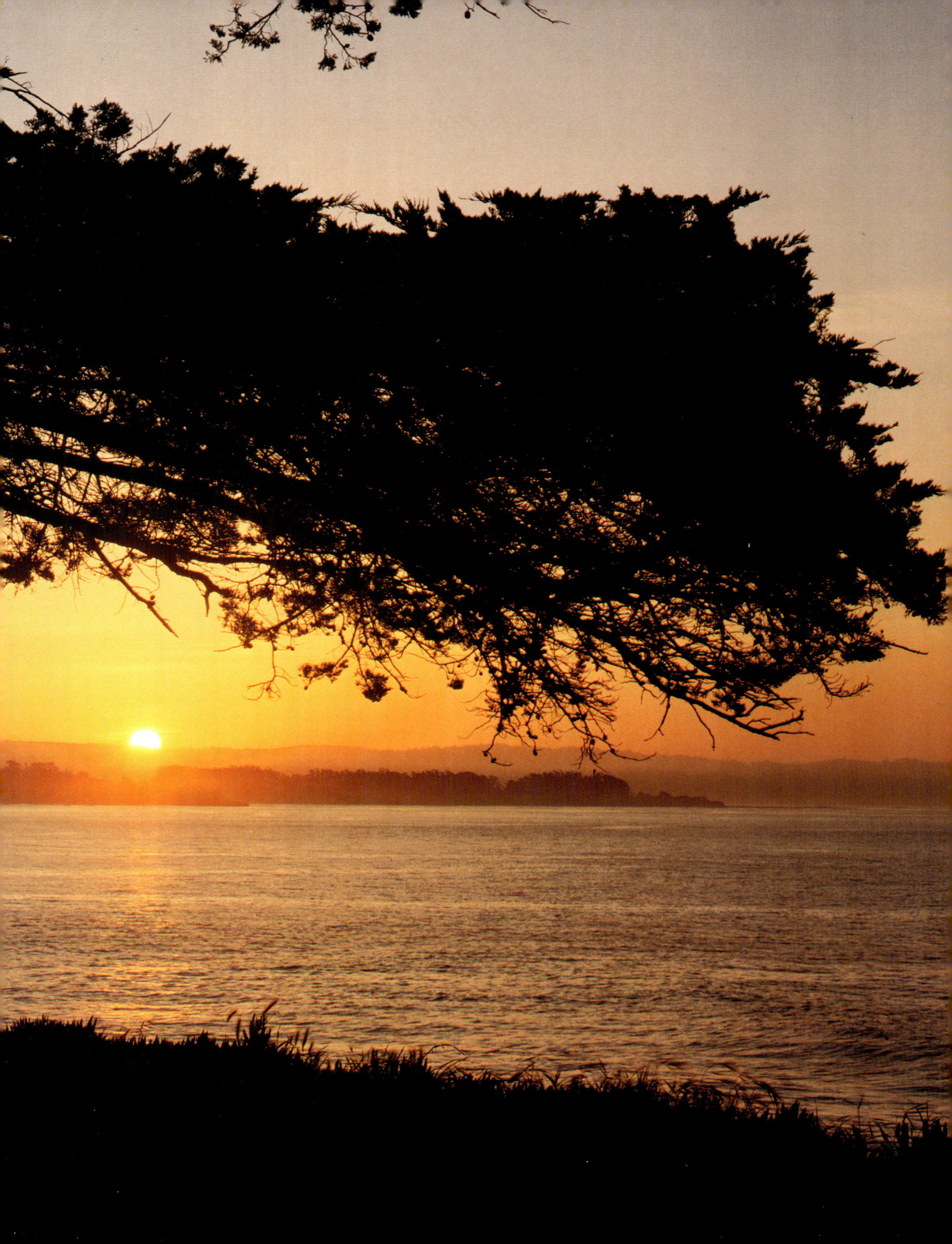

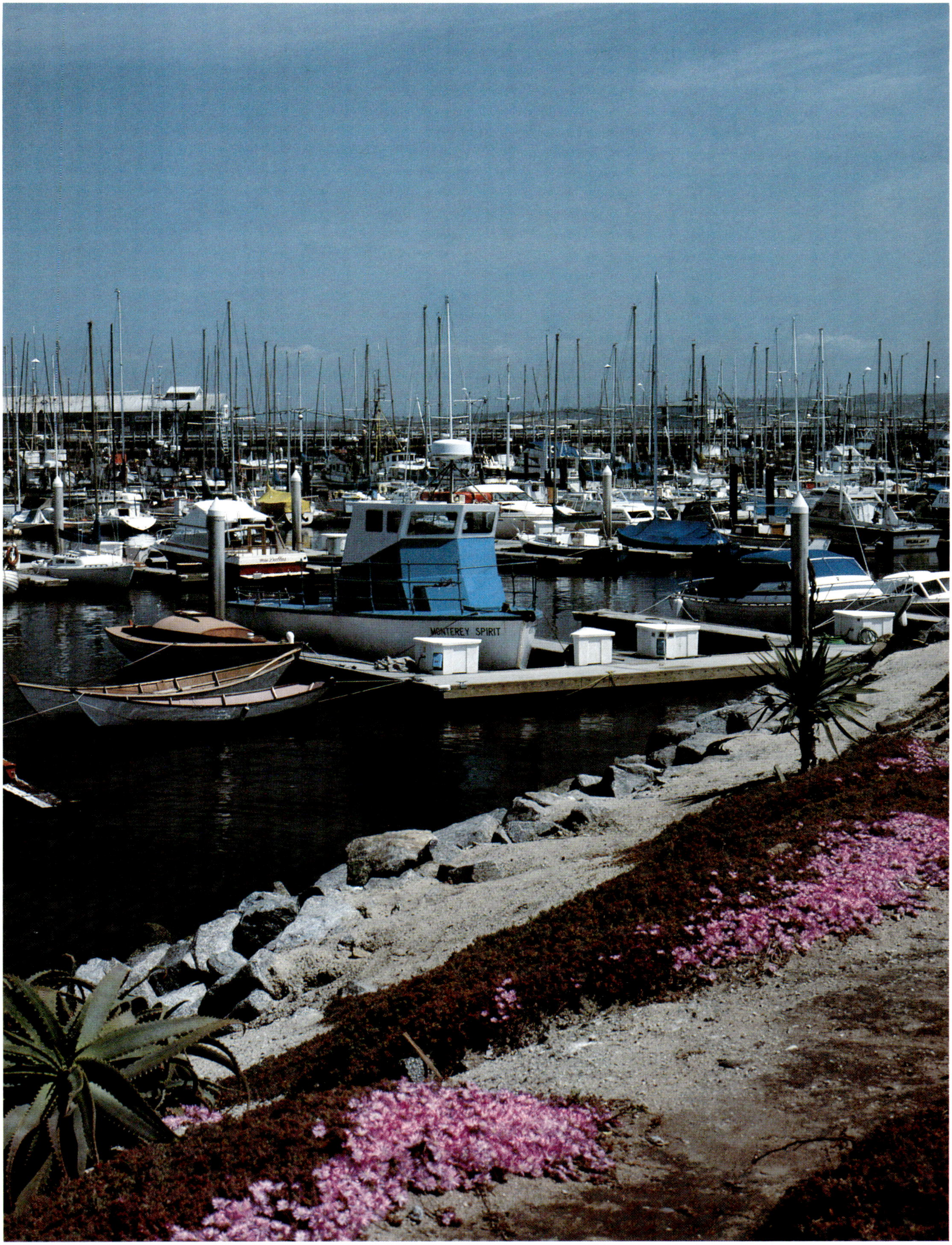
MONTEREY SPIRIT

Big Sur coastline

Monterey Harbor

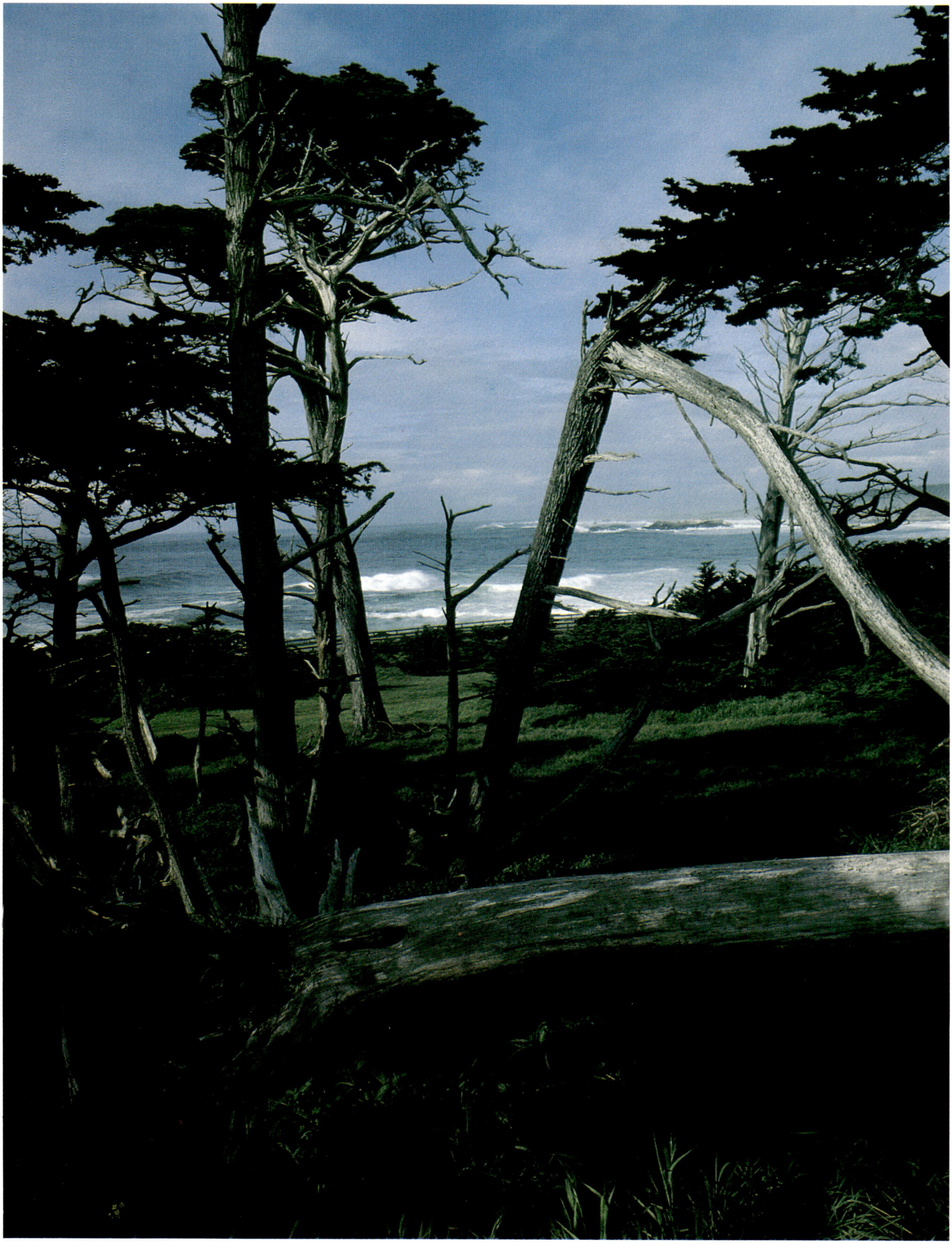

Pigeon Point Lighthouse

The view from Seventeen Mile Drive

Carmelite Mission

30

The coastline south of Big Sur

Remember the smell and the wind →

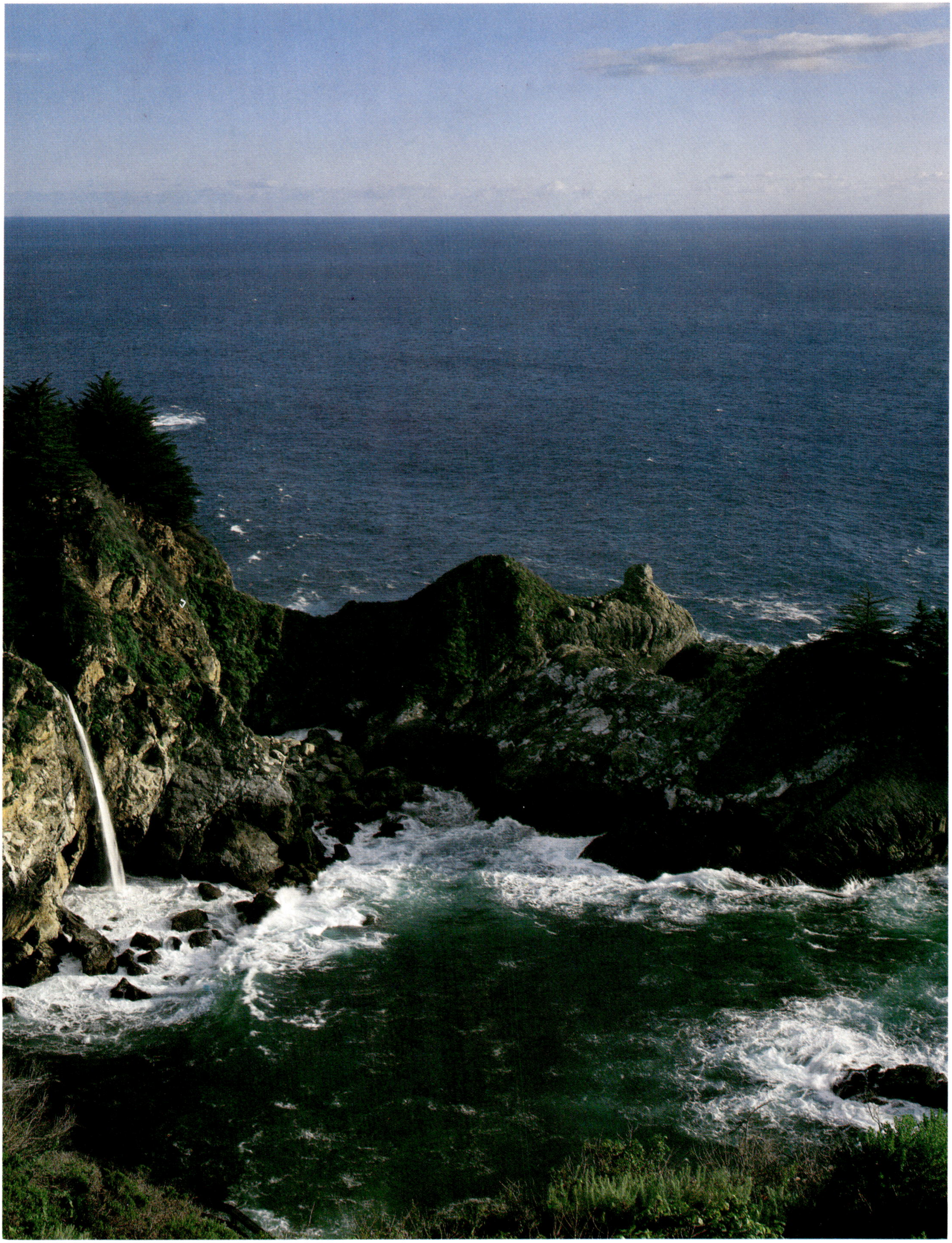

Seals off of Santa Cruz

Flowers along the Big Sur Highway

32

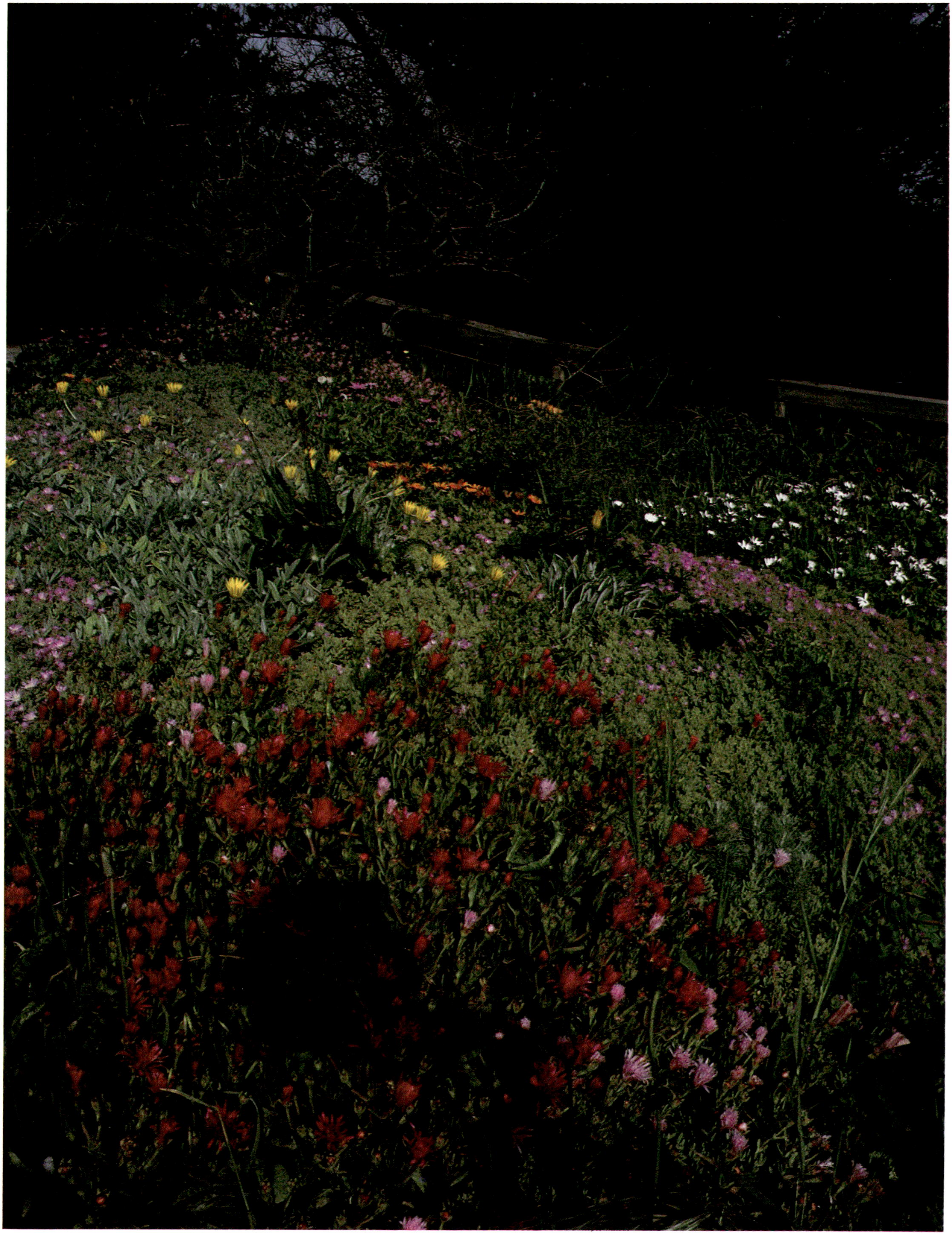

Carmel Bay

Roaring Camp in Felton

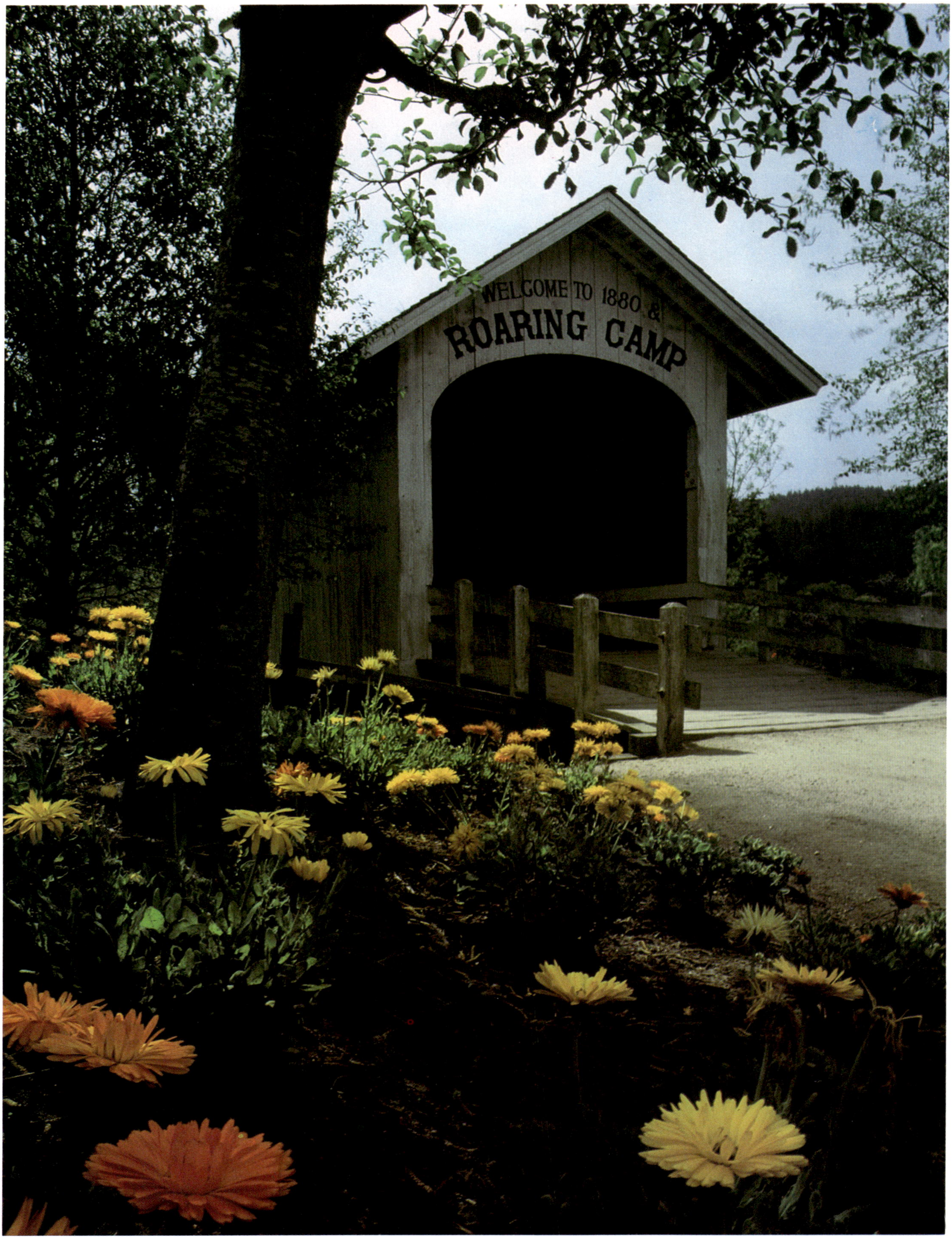
WELCOME TO 1880 &
ROARING CAMP

Santa Cruz Boardwalk

Big Sur coastline

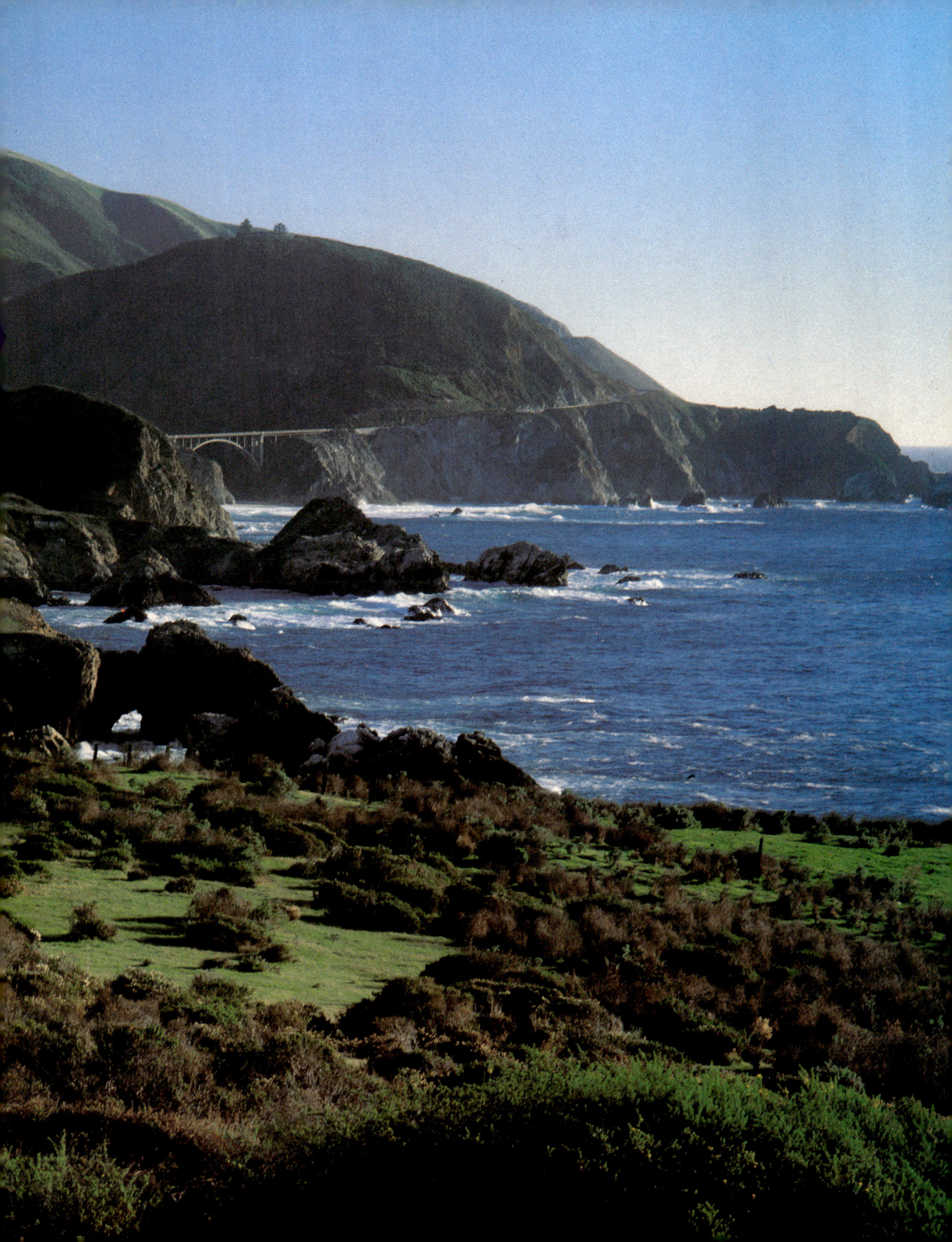

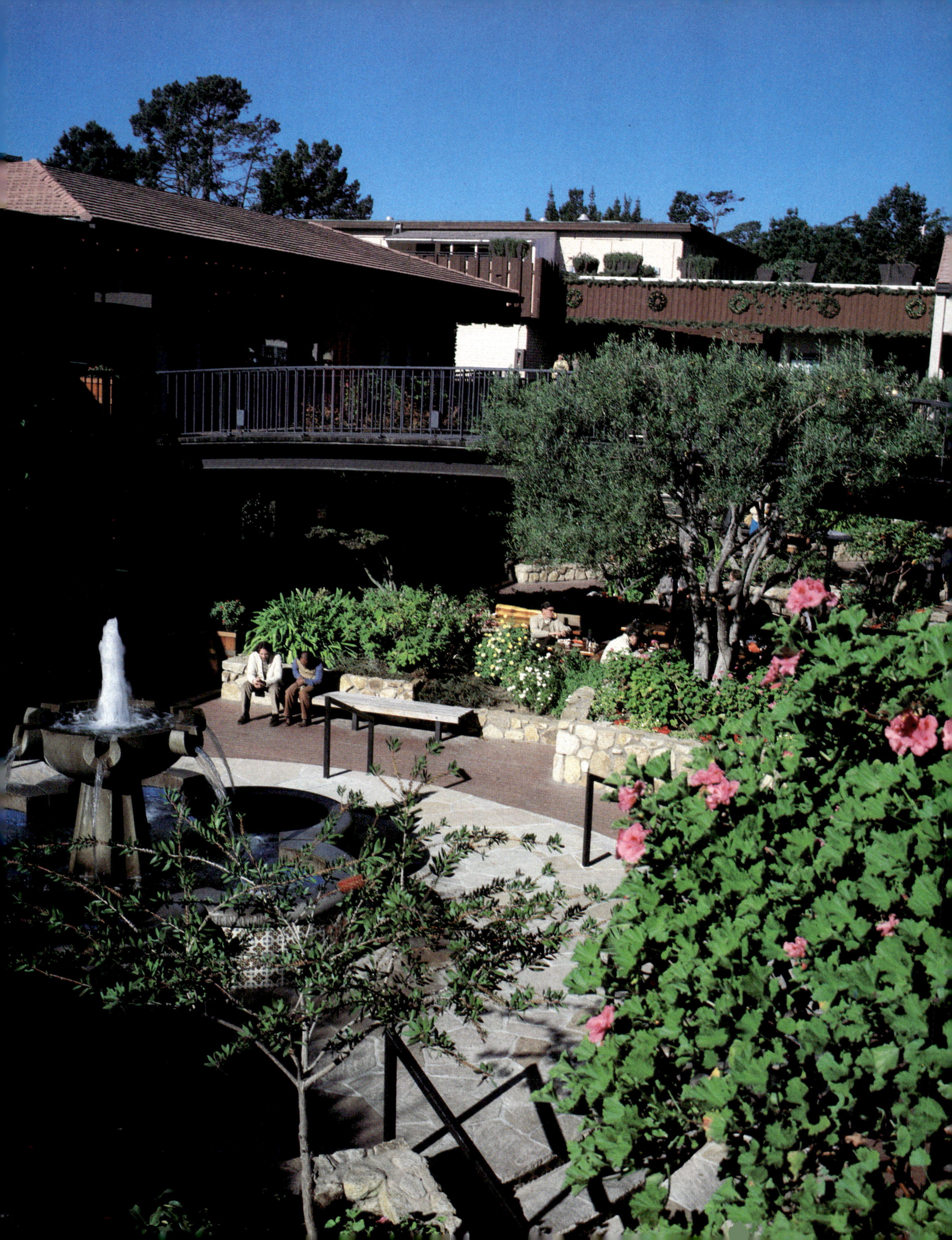

*Big Sur coastline
(Following pages) South Monterey Bay*

Shopping Plaza in Carmel

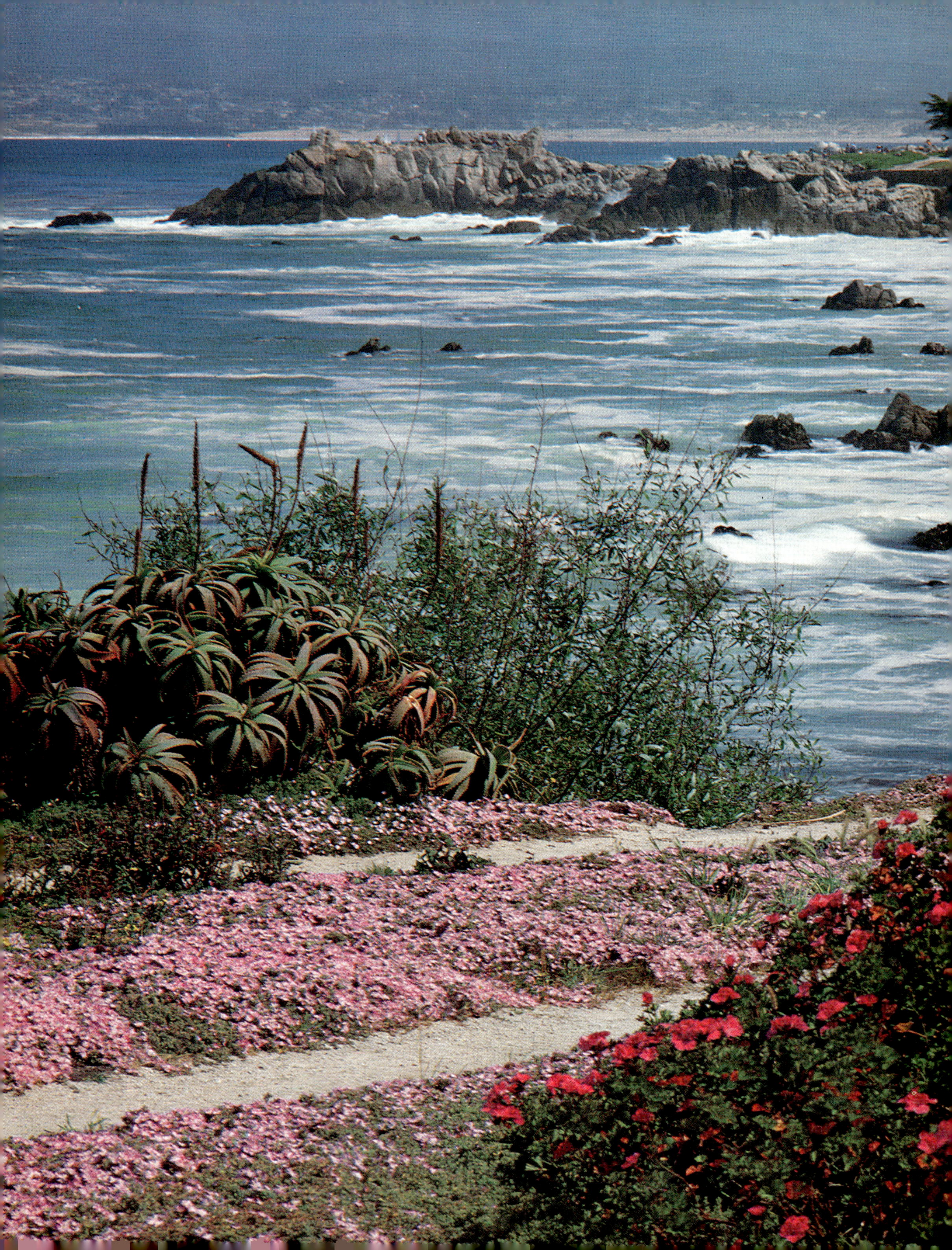

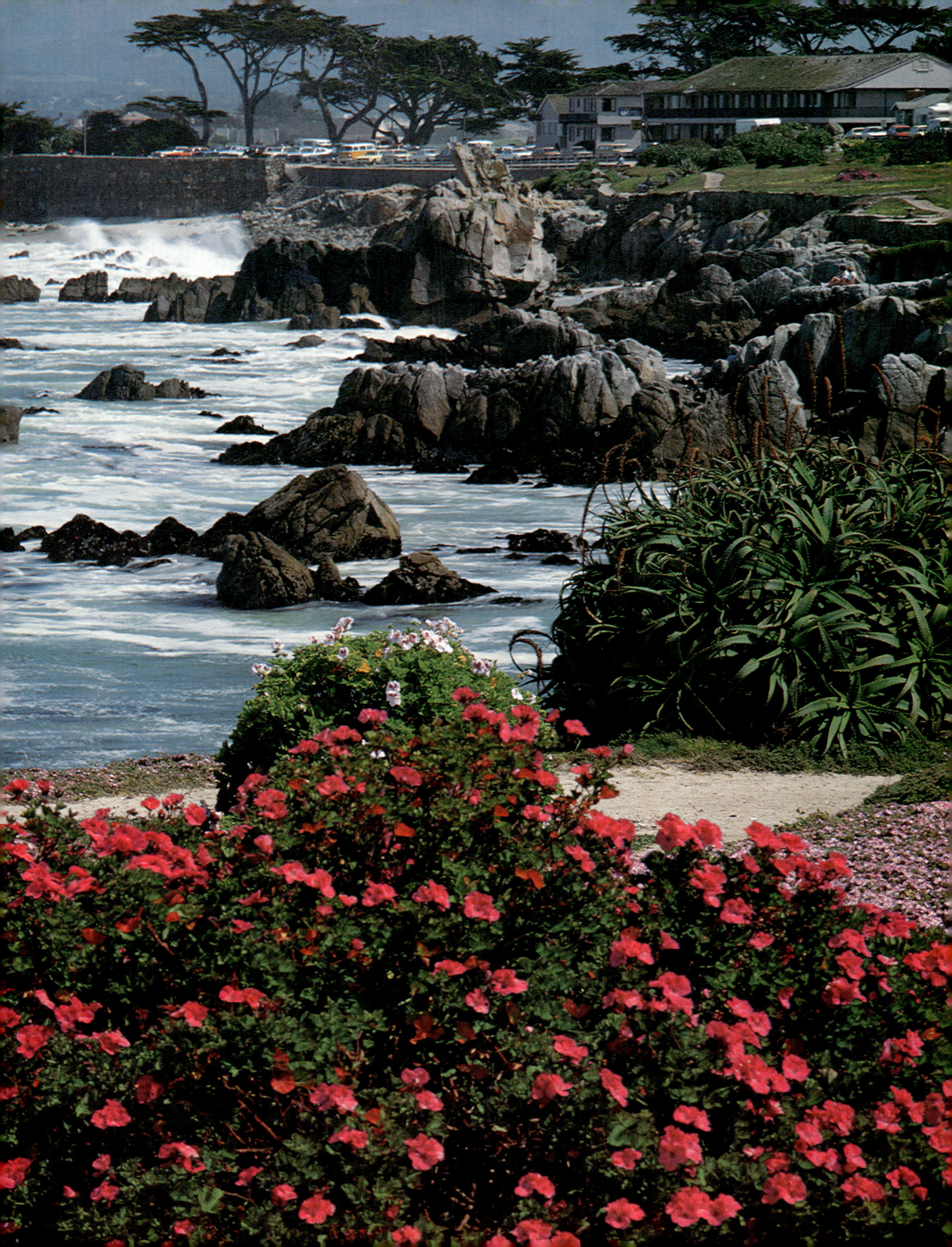

Big Sur coastline

Carmelite Mission

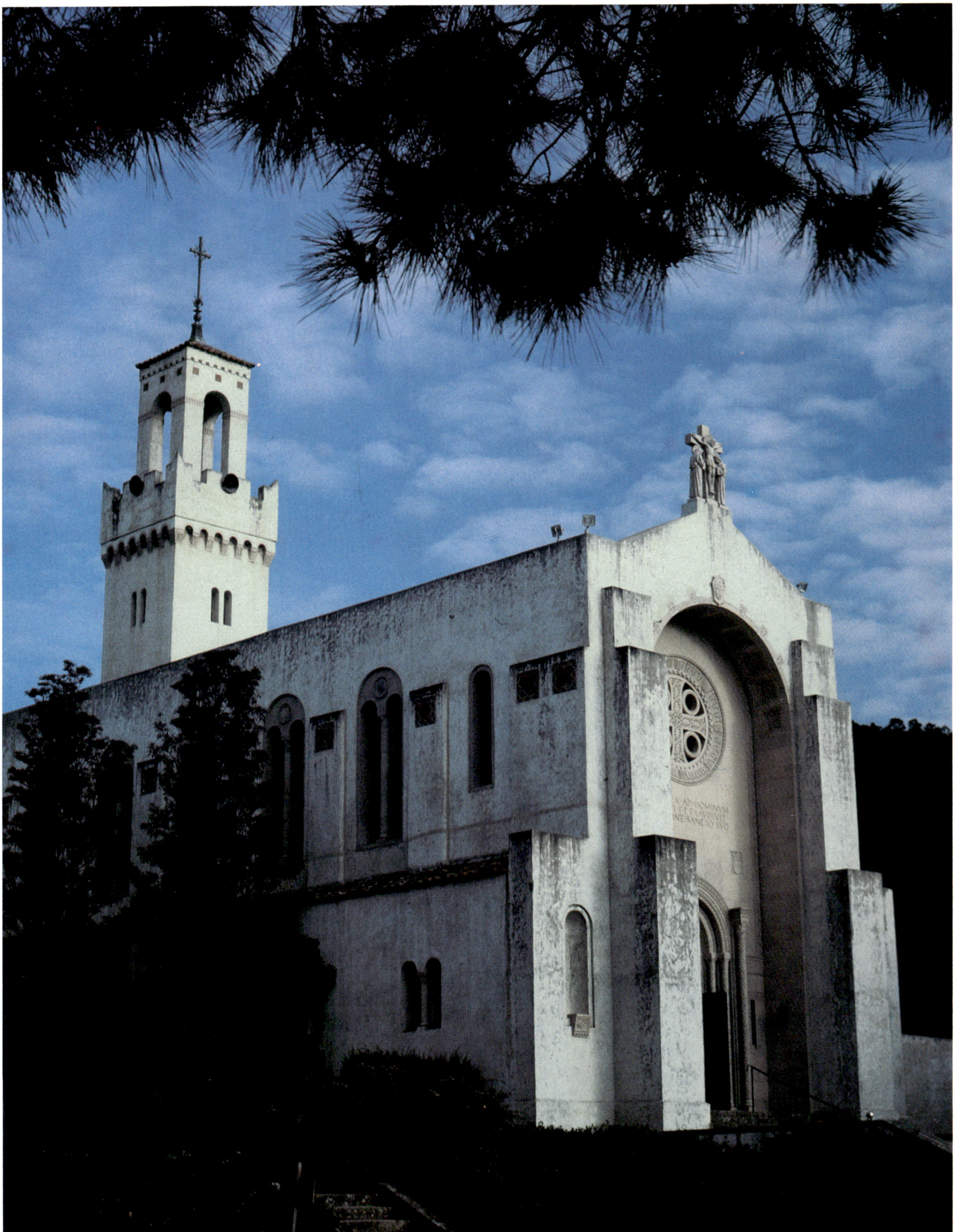

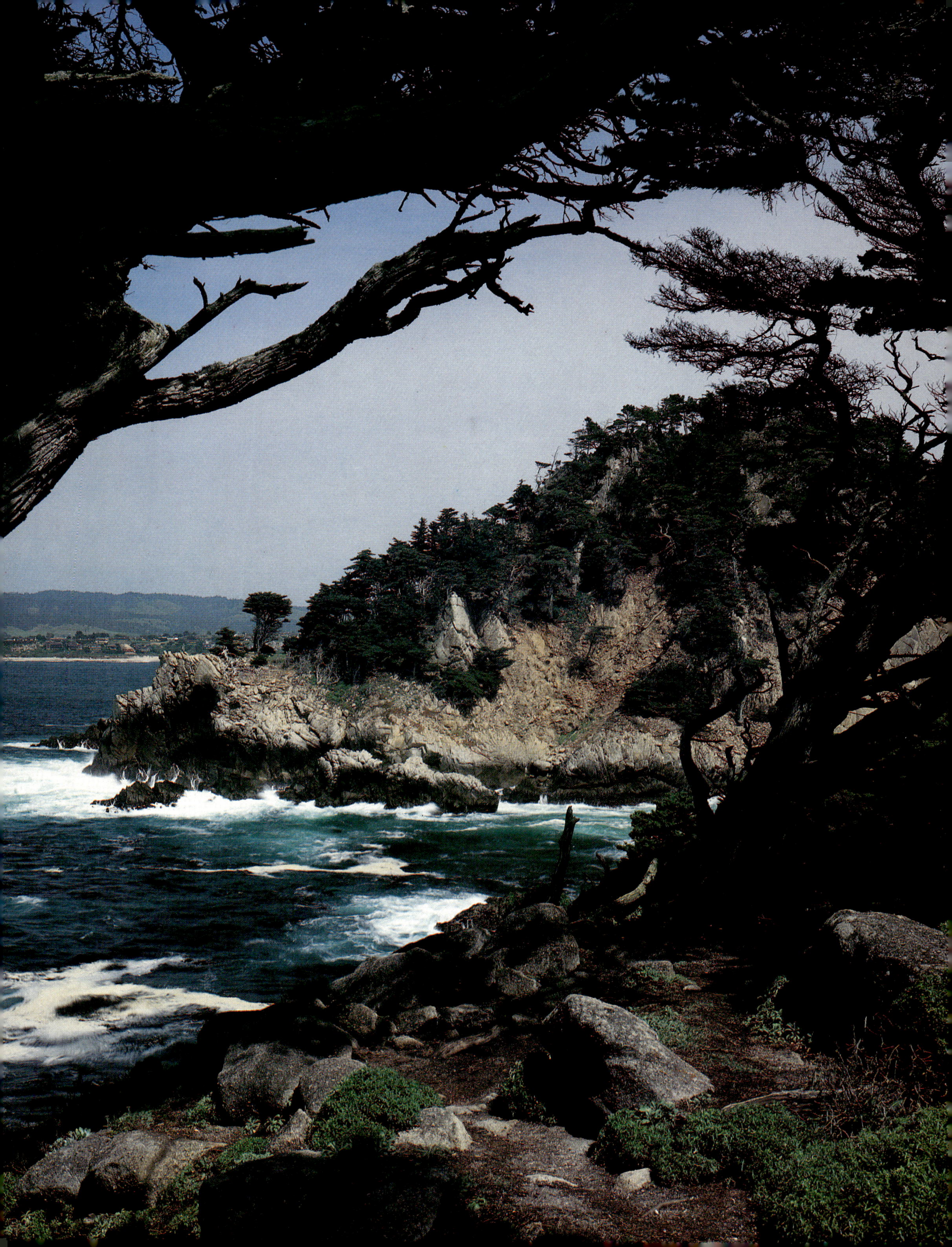

Footpath along South Monterey Bay

Big Dome and Cypress Cove, Point Lobos

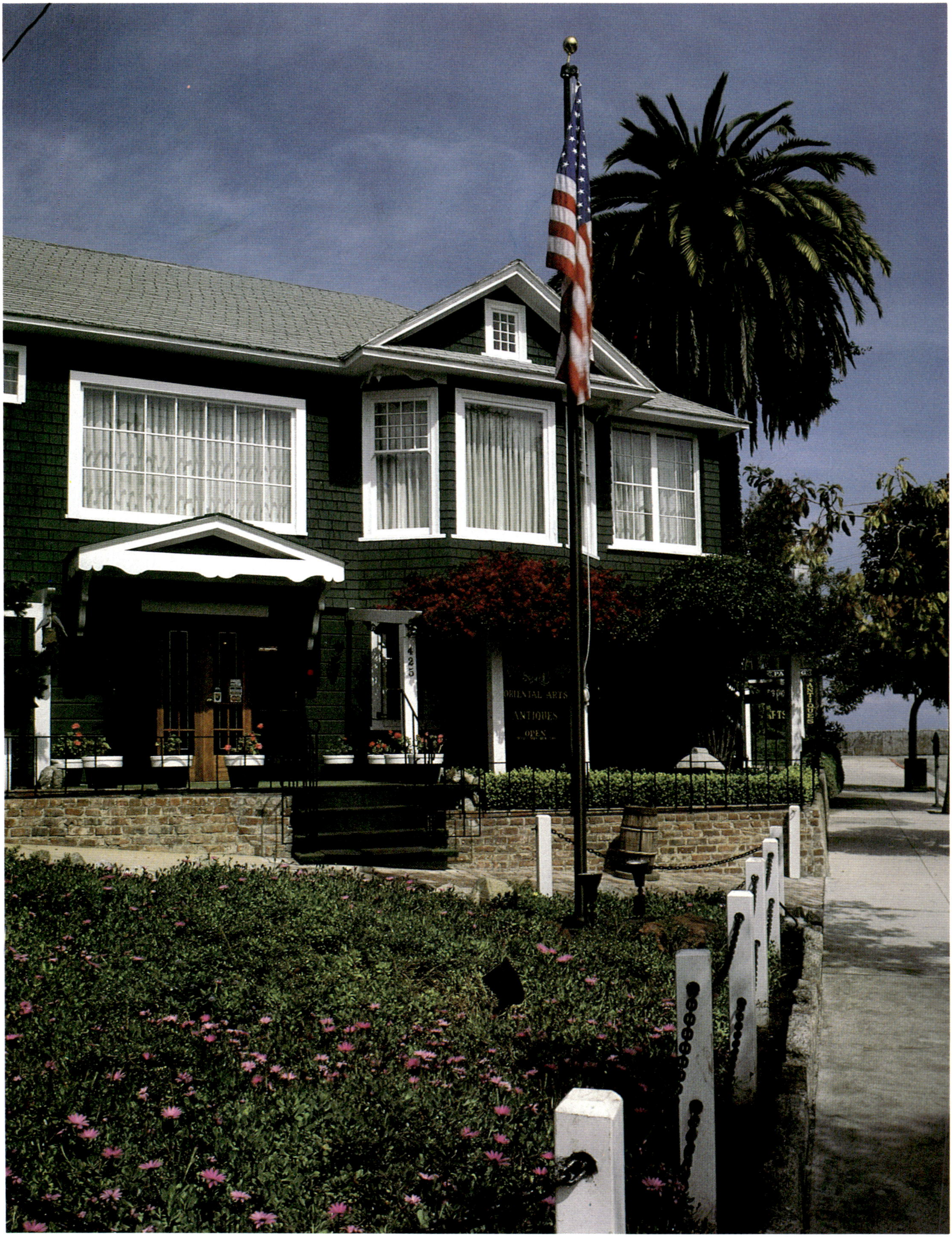
425
ORIENTAL ARTS
ANTIQUES
OPEN
ANTIQUES

Store at Monterey Harbor

Monterey Harbor

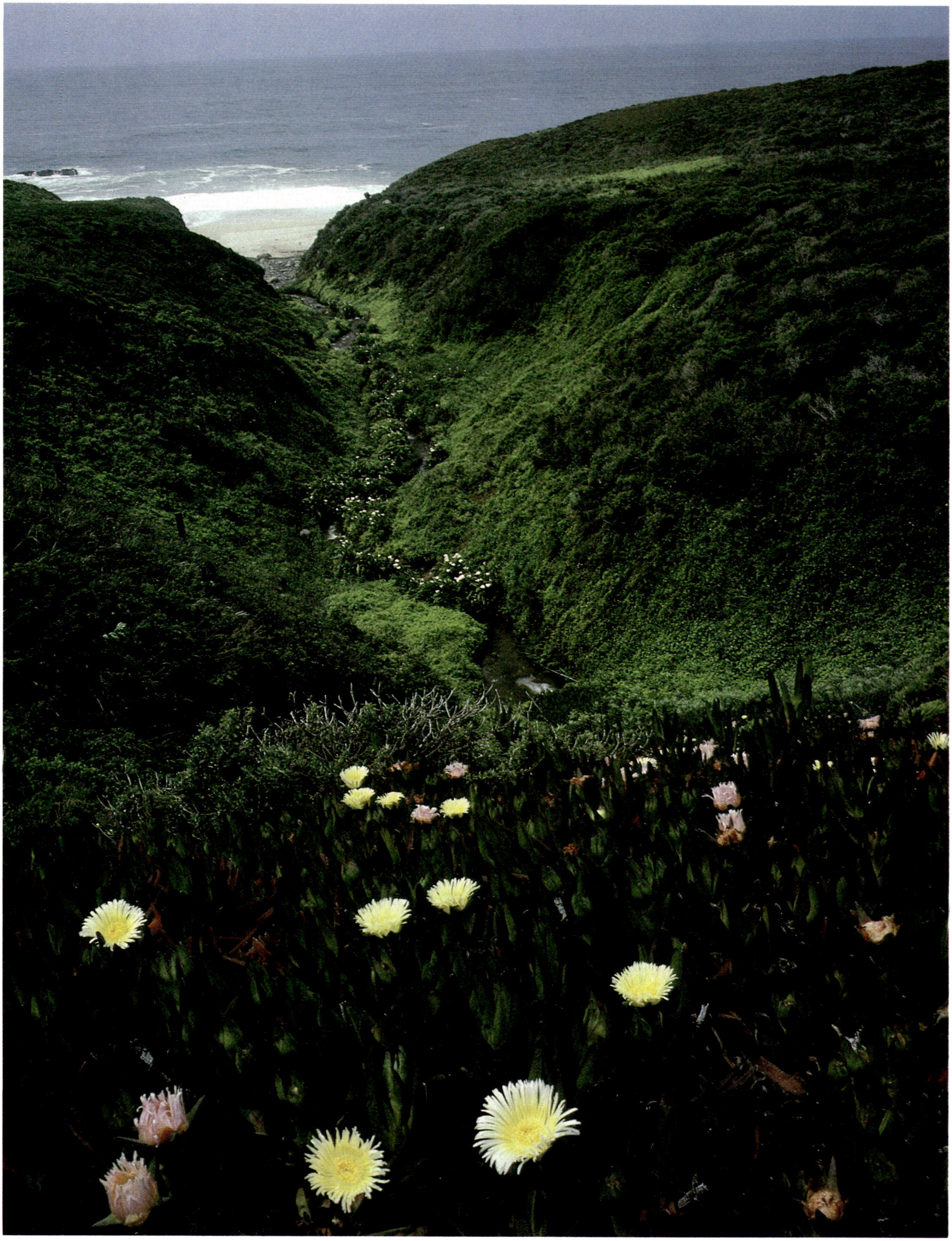

Fisherman's Wharf, Monterey

Creek along the Big Sur Highway

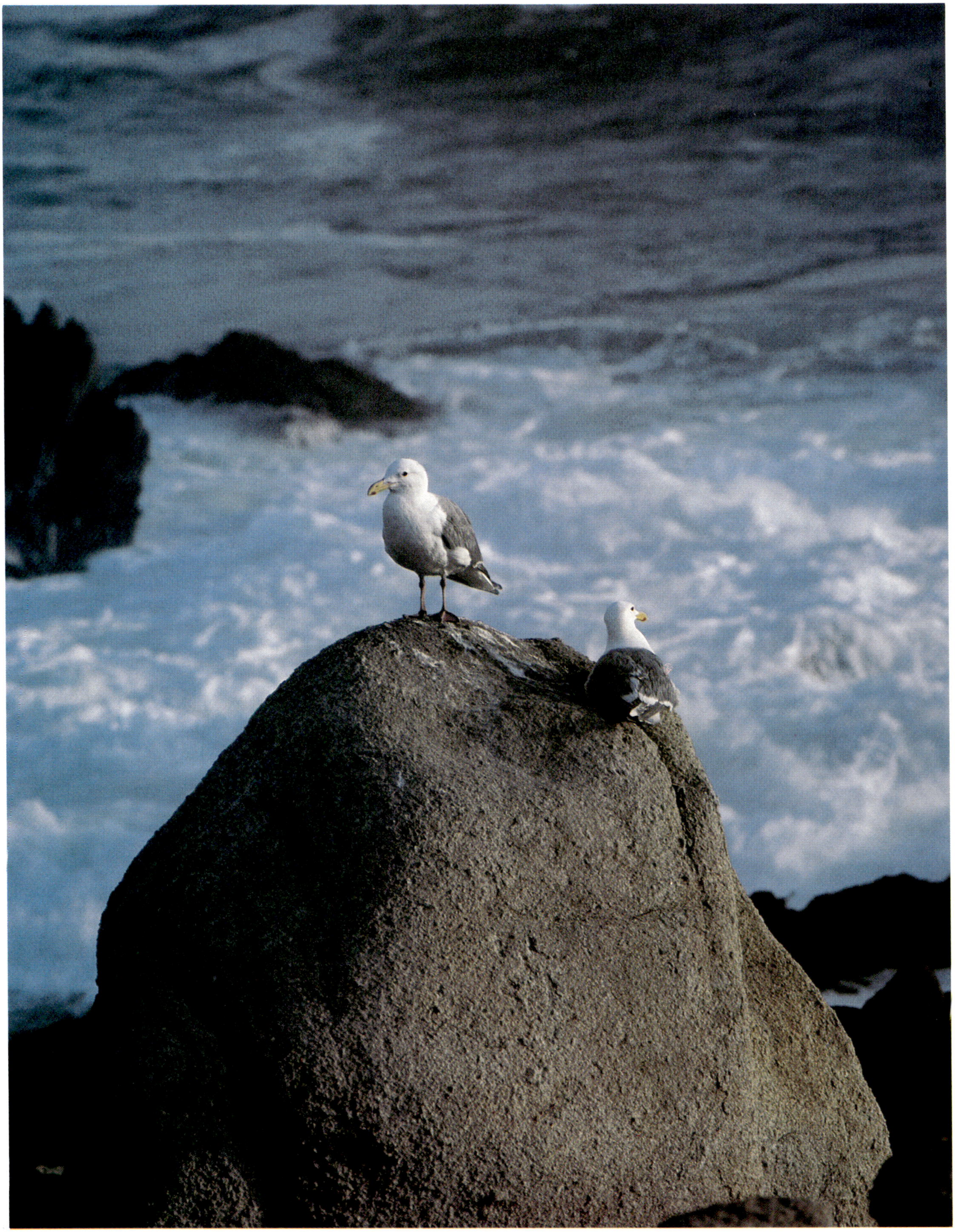

Seagulls at Monterey Bay

Monterey Bay
(Following page) The coastline south of Carmel Highlands
(Second following page) Carmel Mission

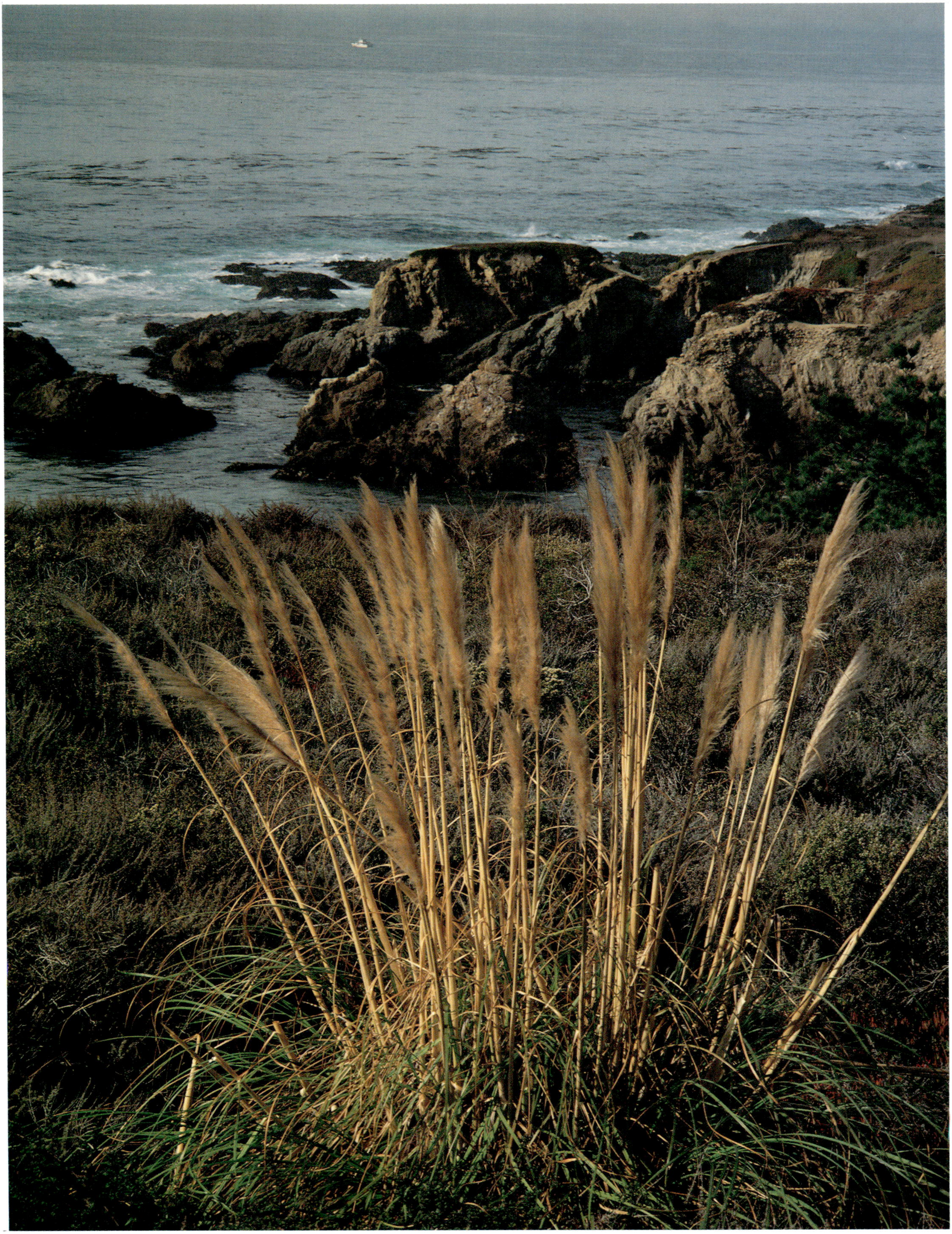

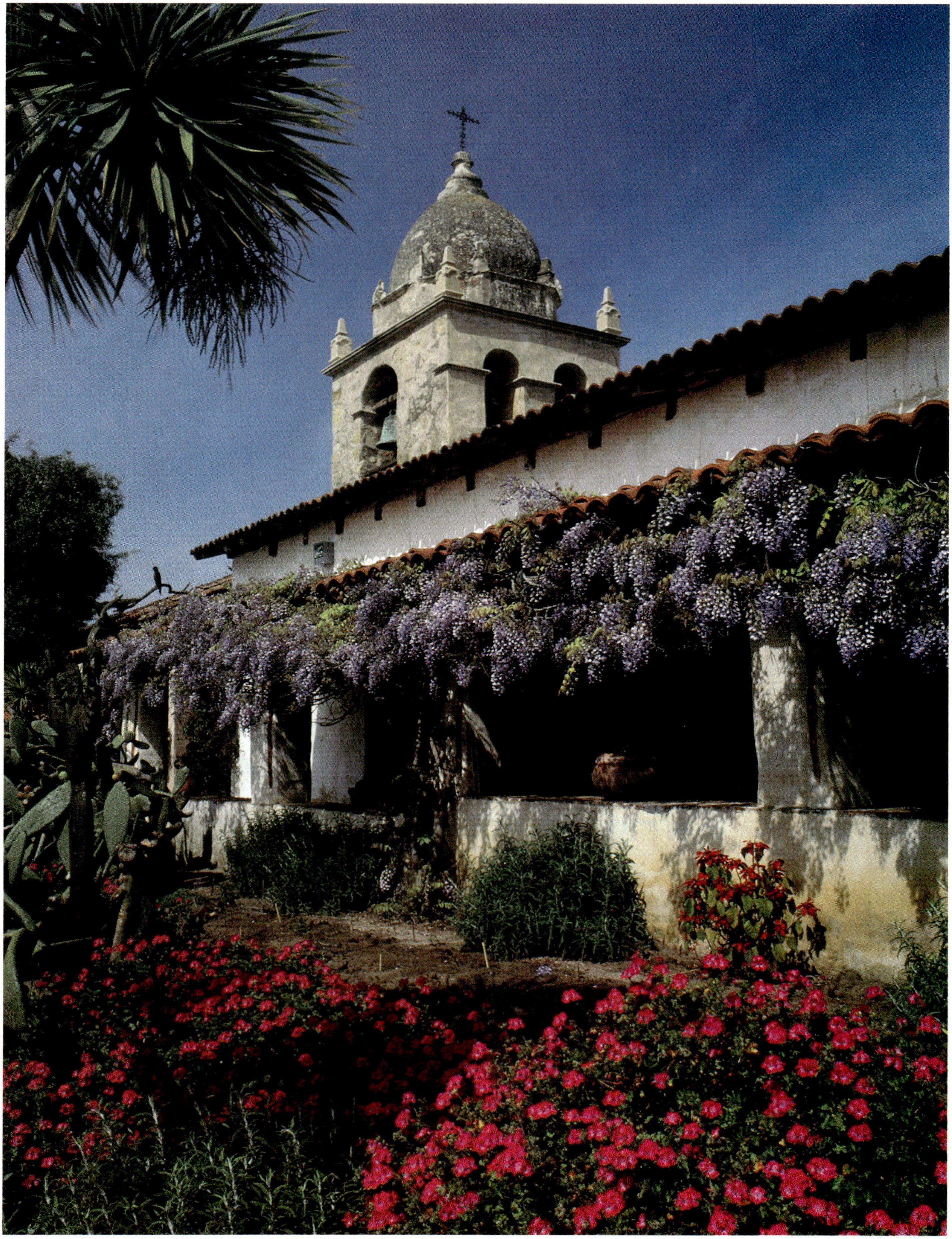

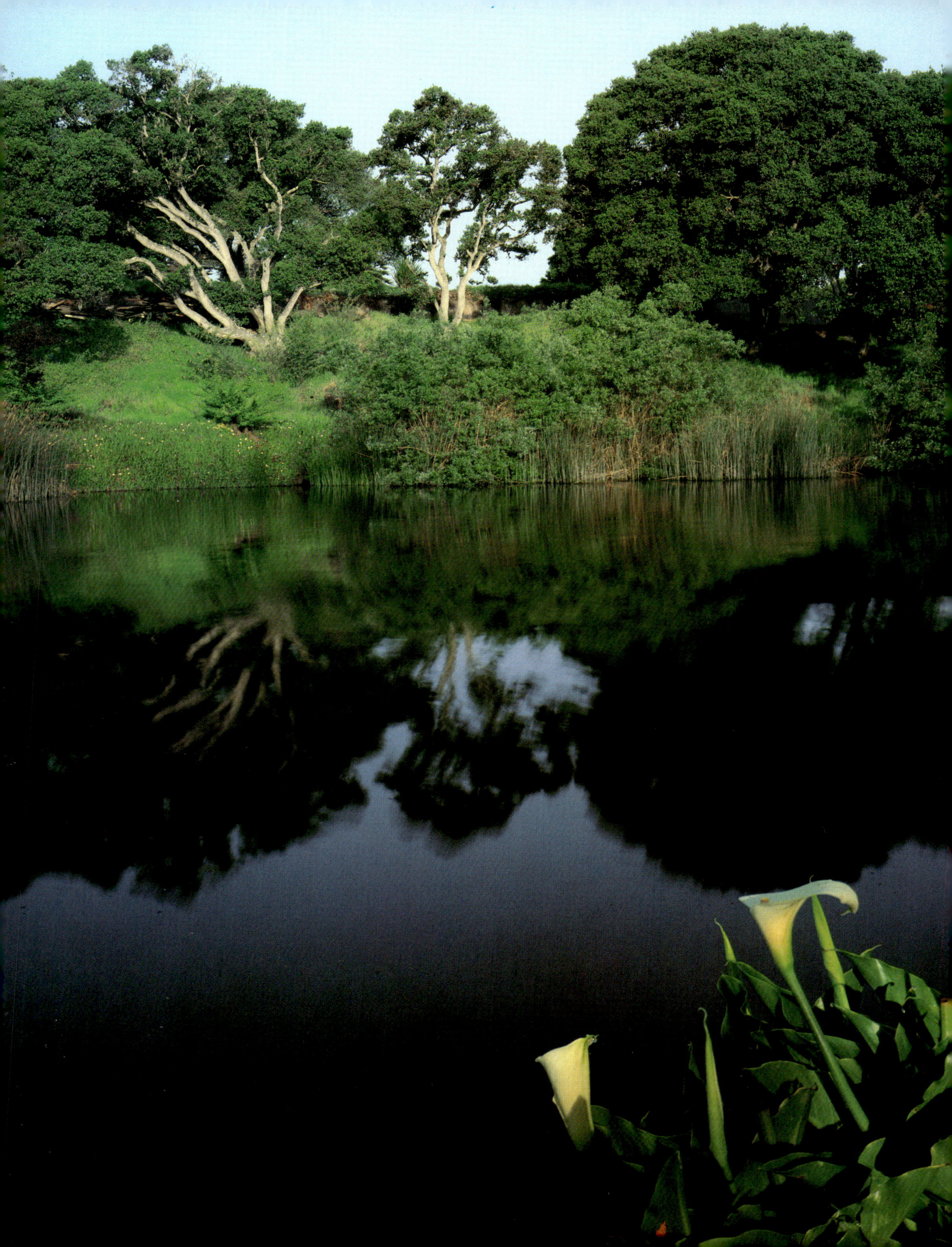

Monterey Harbor
(Following pages) Lone cypress at Monterey Bay

El Estero Lake in Monterey

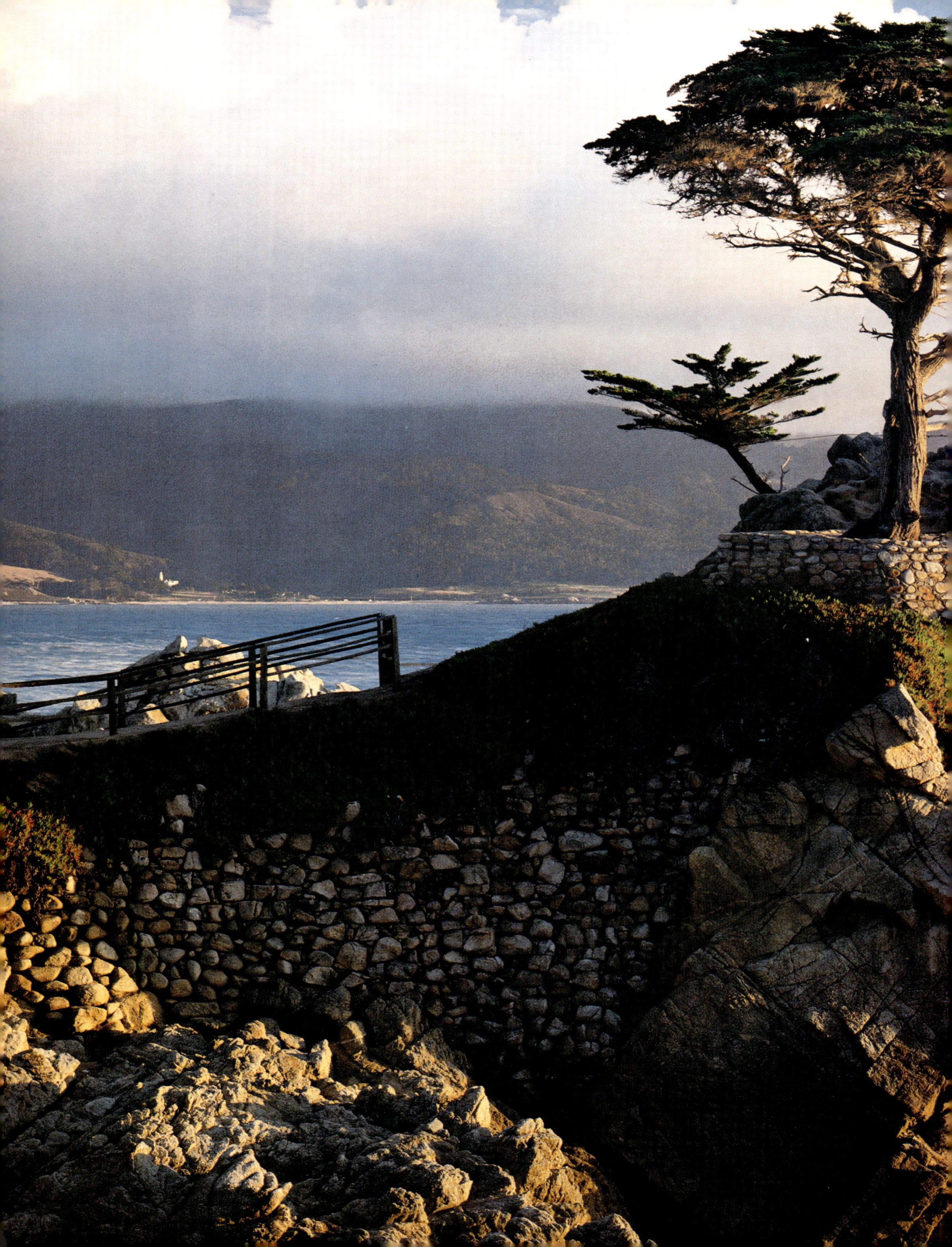

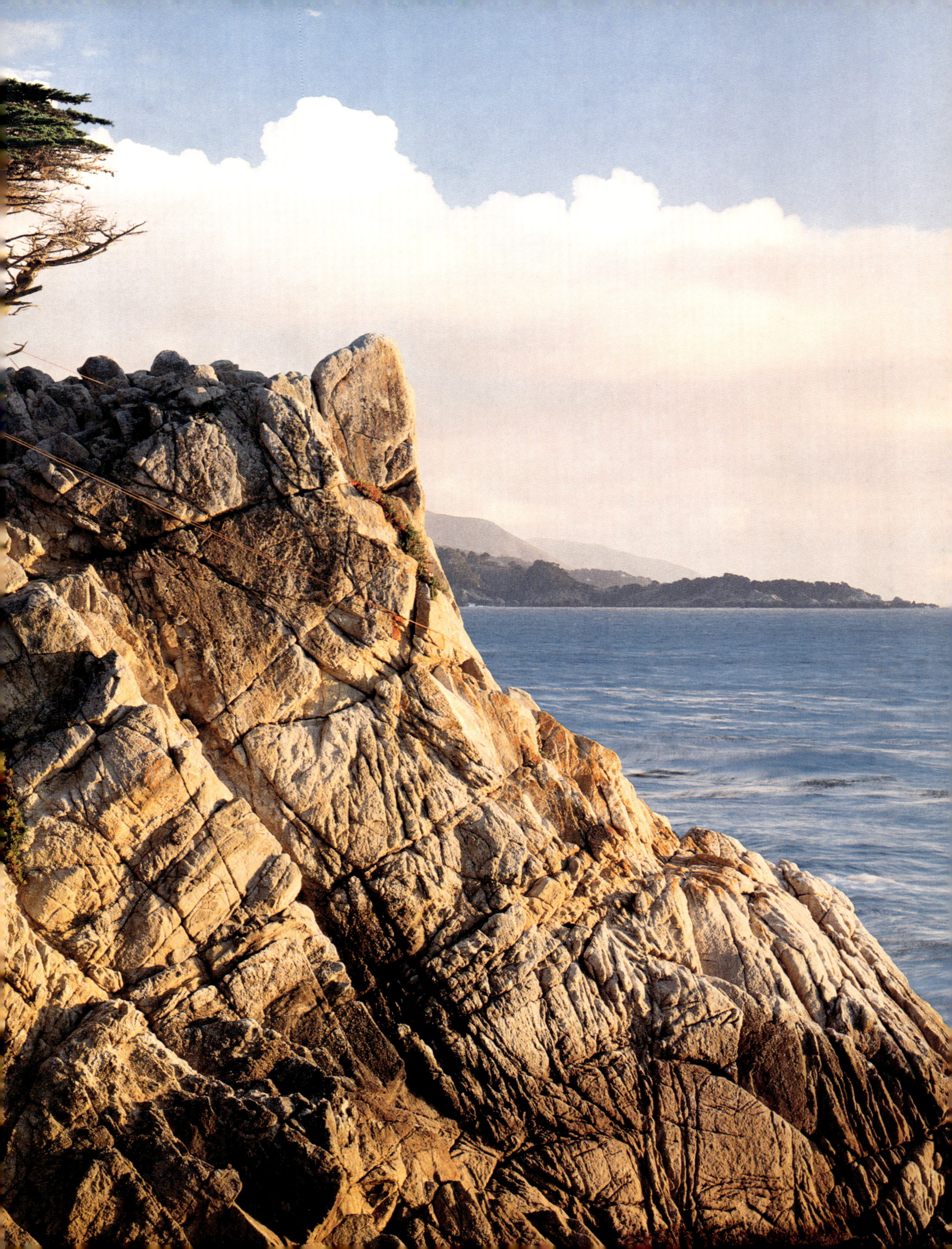

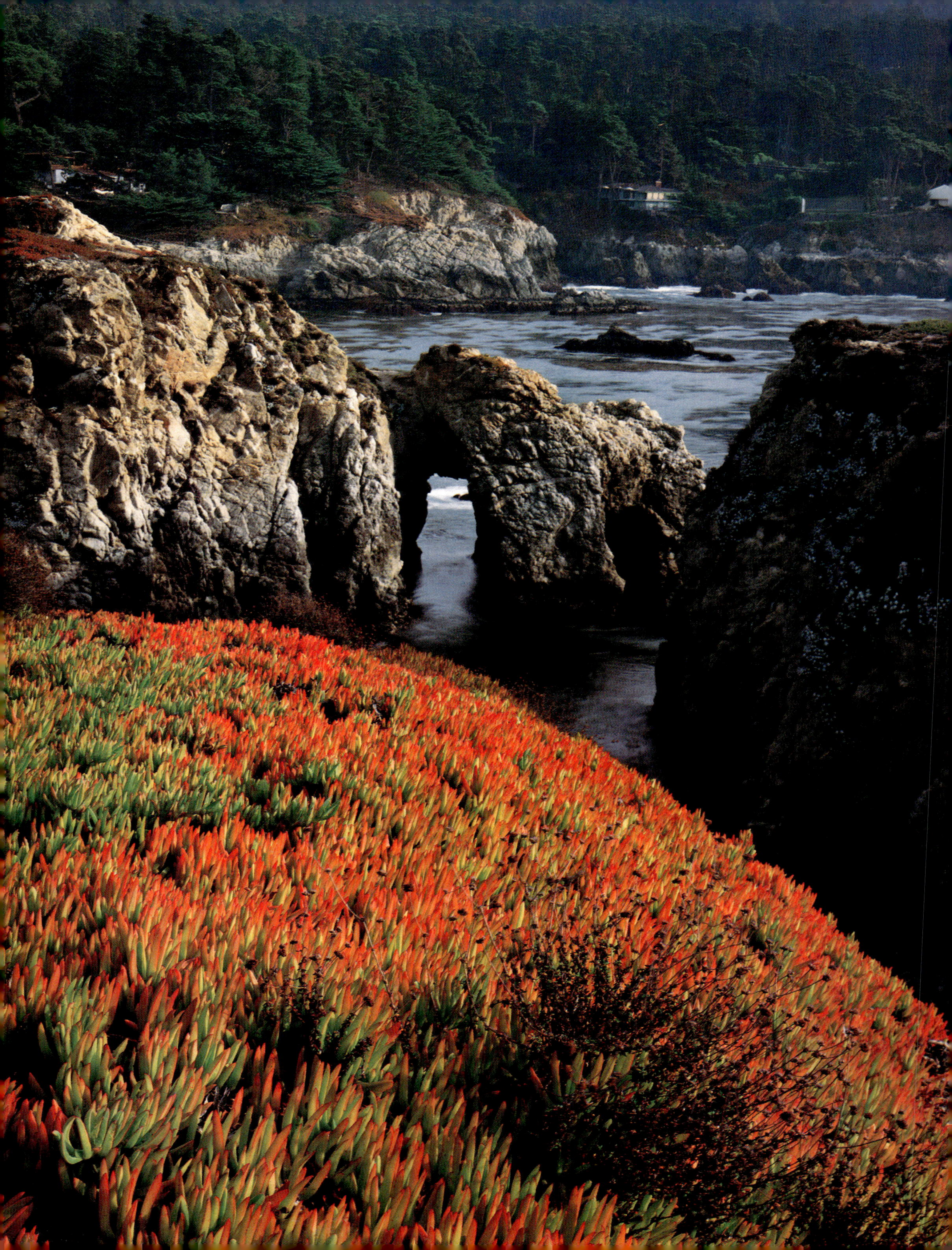

A century plant at Monterey Bay
(Following page) Big Sur coastline

Point Lobos

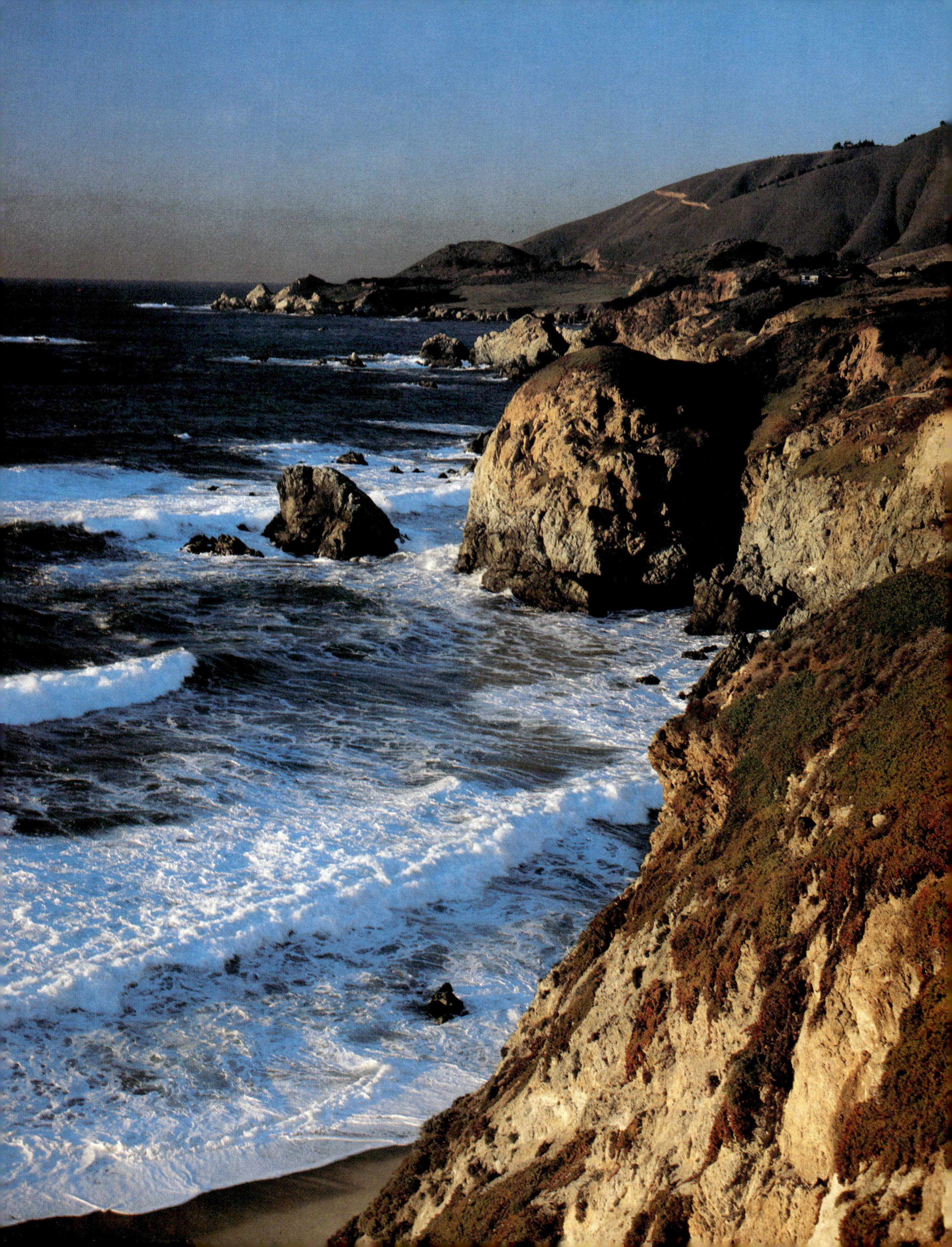

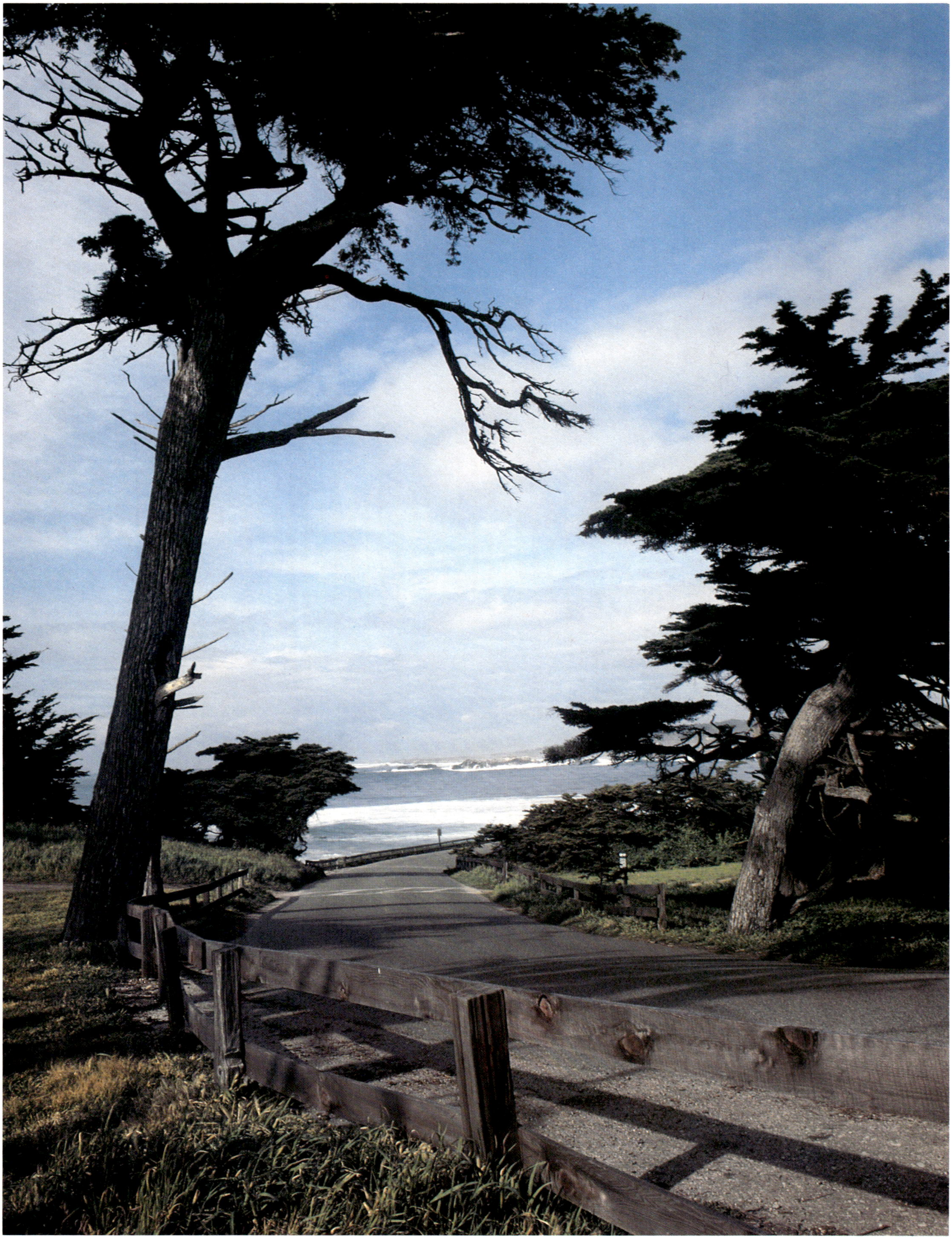

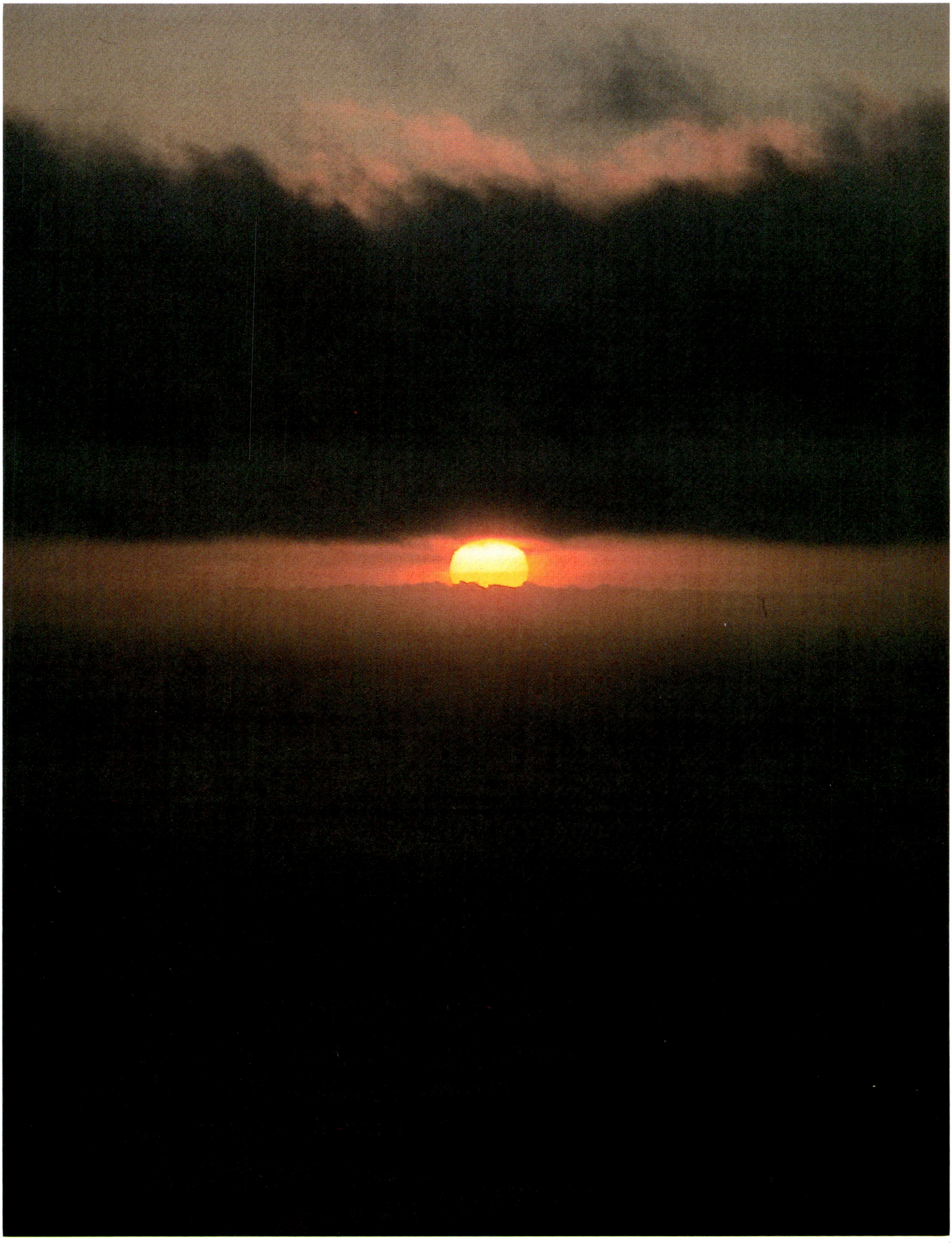

Big Sur coastline

Pigeon Point Lighthouse
(Preceding page) Seventeen Mile Drive

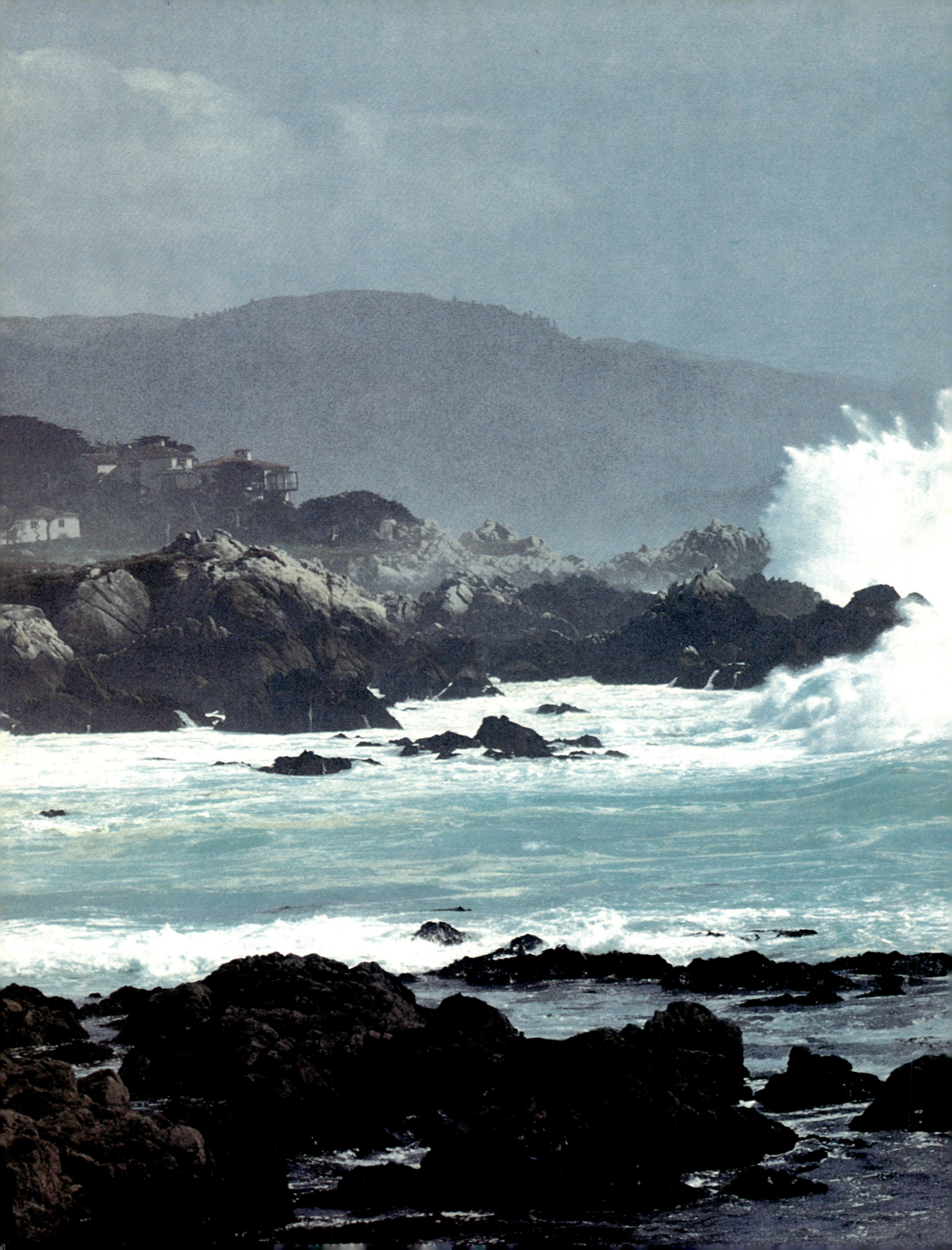

a few Bohemians from San Francisco came to settle, building their dwellings within a fragrant forest of pines that overlooked a beach of white, sparkling sands. Although the town has not entirely escaped the commercial developments that seem always to follow in the wake of any area's expanding popularity, it has yet preserved an atmosphere of "small town-ness" through ordinances prohibiting large buildings.

A stroll through the village will reveal to the visitor what Carmel-by-the-Sea has become famous for—its many art galleries. More than 50 of these establishments are contained within an area of less than one square mile. In addition to showing the works of hundreds of full-time and part-time artists, some galleries also carry the works of recognized creative giants, such as Henry Moore, Chagall, and Delacroix.

Restaurants here seem as abundant as galleries, their menus featuring the finest in international cuisines. Many of the smaller restaurants can be found within the four levels of the beautifully landscaped Carmel Plaza, which also houses many unusual gift and craft shops.

One will note that the town has a plaza-like feel, containing a number of parks and trees, which tend to overhang the city's streets. Due to city ordinances, outside the business district there are no neon signs cluttering the view; there is no noise from jukeboxes disturbing the calm; no buildings more than two stories high shading the sunny thoroughfares. Neither will one find parking meters to gulp one's last bit of change. Add to this list no courthouse, no jail, and no cemetery, and the visitor begins to understand the Carmel resident's aversion to things that really represent "big town-ness."

Before leaving the area, one can view a preserved piece of the Monterey Peninsula's Spanish beginnings by visiting the Carmel Mission, located in the Carmel Valley alongisde the Carmel River. Founded originally in 1770, on a site in Monterey, the church was later moved to Carmel. A complete restoration program began in 1934. The structure still has much of the same appearance as when first erected, with walls of sandstone five feet thick, which protect an interior containing many of the mission's original paintings and statues.

Combine the pleasures found in exploring the Peninsula's scenic and historical pathways, together with its superb recreational opportunities—tennis, swimming, sailing, scuba diving, fishing, horseback riding, golfing, and hunting—and one quickly understands the enormous popularity of this paradise by the Pacifc.

View from Seventeen Mile Drive

The Peninsula in Literature

The pictures in this book have depicted in colorful detail the surface beauty of the Monterey Peninsula. But there is a unique quality to this region that sometimes escapes the impartial lens of the camera. It is an essence that can only be captured in the words of those who have absorbed the Peninsula's ambience and in moments of inspiration, have given those printed words to the world.

Of the many early spokesmen for the Peninsula's natural excellence, perhaps the most famous was the poet Robinson Jeffers. Arriving here in 1914, he was immediately overcome by the magnificence of the unspoiled scenery. It did not take long for Jeffers to choose the Peninsula as a permanent homesite, and he promptly started construction on Tor House—a project that would consume him for the next five years. Where he built his granite structure on Carmel Point, Jeffers also planted cypress and eucalyptus trees, and in a moment of reflection on what he had created with his own hands, he wrote:

>If you should look for this place after a handful of lifetimes:
>Perhaps of my planted forest a few
>May stand yet, dark-leaved Australians or the coast cypress,
>   haggard
>With storm-drift; but fire and axe are devils.
>Look for foundations of sea-worn granite, my fingers had the
>   art
>To make stone love stone, you will find some remnant.

In his poem ''Tamar,'' portions of which convey the beauty of the Peninsula as few other writings have, Jeffers paints a verbal portrait of his immense love for this land, saying:

>. . . do you remember at all
>The beauty and strangeness of this place? Old cypresses
>The Sailor wind works into deep-sea knots. . . .
>Water that owns the north and west and south
>and is all colors and never is all quiet,

> And the fogs are its breath and float along the branches of
>   the cypresses.
> And I forgot the coals of ruby lichen
> That glow in the fog on the old twigs. To live here
> Seventy-five years or eighty, and have children,
> and watch these things fill up their eyes, would not
> Be a bad life. . . .

Born in Salinas, California, John Steinbeck used locations familiar to him in the hills and valleys of Central California as backgrounds for many of his novels. Cannery Row held a special fascination for him with its assortment of colorful characters, those individuals that live "on the fringes of society." He observed the mixture of nationalities who answered the call of the screaming cannery whistles whenever a boatload of sardines pulled into the bay, "men and women in trousers and rubber coats and oil-cloth aprons . . . running to clean and cut and pack and cook and can the fish."

While the city slept, Steinbeck would walk the area of the canneries, absorbing the atmosphere that surrounded them during the early morning hours—a time, wrote Steinbeck, when "the Row seems to hang suspended out of time in the silvery light. The street lights go out, and the weeds are a brilliant green. The corrugated iron of the canneries glows with the pearly lucence of platinum or old pewter. . . . And the rush and drag of the waves can be heard as they splash in among the piles of the canneries. It is a time of great peace, a deserted time, a little era of rest."

On his trip to California in 1879-1880, Robert Louis Stevenson stopped for a time in Monterey. Little more than a century had passed since the town's settling, and Stevenson found its people still practicing their ancient customs. The buildings, too, had changed little, construction coming almost to a standstill some 30 years earlier, when the greater portion of Monterey's population left to seek their fortunes in the gold fields.

> "The town," noted Stevenson, "was a place of two or three streets, economically paved with sea-sand, and two or three lanes, which were water-courses in the rainy season, and at all times were rent up by fissures four or five feet deep. There were no street lights. Short sections of wooden sidewalk only added to the dangers of the night, for they were often high above the level of the roadway, and no one could tell where they would be likely to begin or end. The houses were for the most part built of unbaked adobe brick, many of them old for so new a country, some of very elegant proportions, with low, spacious, shapely rooms, and walls so thick that the heat of summer never dried them to the heart."

Fascinated by the action of the waves breaking against the land, Stevenson would watch the surf for long hours, noting its changing forms and listening to its ageless song. "The waves," he wrote, "which lap so quietly about the jetties of Monterey grow louder and larger in the distance; you can see the breakers leaping high and white by day; at night, the outline of the shore is traced in transparent silver by the moonlight and the flying foam; and from all around, even in quiet weather, the low, distant, thrilling roar of the Pacific hangs over the coast and the adjacent country like smoke above a battle.''

In 1904 a group of young artists and writers began erecting houses among the pines that bordered a cove of Carmel Bay. Here they established ''The Village,'' later to be known as Carmel-by-the-Sea. One of this group, the author Mary Austin, recalled in later years the look of early Carmel: ''. . . when I first came to this land, a virgin thicket of buckthorn sage and sea-blue lilac spread between well-spaced, long-leaved pines. The dunes glistened white with violet shadows, and in warm hollows, between live oaks, the wine of light had mellowed undisturbed a thousand years . . . .''

Freed of the clamor and demands of city life—from which all these early settlers had fled—there was time for ''talk—ambrosial, unquotable talk,'' and walks in the woods, surrounded by beauty. ''But I think that the memorable and now vanished charm of Carmel,'' continued Austin, ''lay, perhaps, most in the reality of the simplicity attained, a simplicity factually adjusted to the quest of blood and fuel and housing as it can never be in any 'quarter' of city life.''

Beauty of line and profoundness of thought seem the natural result of a writer having sojourned on the Peninsula. But a few of these writers have approached their subject in a more humorous vein, as in this portion of ''The Abalone Song,'' by the poet George Sterling:

> O! Some folks boast of quail on toast,
> Because they think its toney;
> But I'm content to owe rent,
> And live on abalone.
>
> Some stick to biz, some flirt
> Down on the sands at Coney;
> But we, by hell! stay in Carmel
> And nail the abalone.

Mary Austin mourned the passing of the ''old Carmel'' which, by 1927, had begun to attract other seekers of solace. Yet the talents of these new writers and artists only enchanced Carmel's reputation as an oasis of creativity—a place where genius is fed by the constant stimulus of the land's inspiring, natural beauty.

Enlarged Prints

Most of the photography in this book is available as photographic enlargements. Send self-addressed, stamped envelope for information. For a complete product catalog, send $1.00.
Beautiful America Publishing Company
P.O. Box 608
Beaverton, Oregon 97075

1981 Calendars

- Beautiful America
- Beautiful Flowers
- Boston
- California
- Chicago
- Colorado
- Detroit
- Florida
- Great Lakes
- Hawaii
- Illinois
- Los Angeles
- Manhattan
- Massachusetts
- Michigan
- Minnesota
- Missouri
- Mormon Temples
- New England
- New York
- Ohio
- Oregon
- Pennsylvania
- Pittsburgh
- Portland
- San Diego
- San Francisco Bay
- Seattle
- Skiing, U.S.A.
- St. Louis
- Texas
- Virginia
- Volcano, Mt. St. Helens
- Washington
- Washington, D.C.
- Western America
- Western Sailing
- Wisconsin

Beautiful America Publishing Company

The nation's foremost publisher of quality color photography

Current Books

Alaska	Maryland	Oregon Vol. II
Arizona	Massachusetts	Oregon Coast
Boston	Michigan	Oregon Country
British Columbia	Michigan Vol. II	Pacific Coast
California	Minnesota	Pennsylvania
California Vol. II	Missouri	Pittsburgh
California Coast	Montana	San Diego
California Desert	Montana Vol. II	San Francisco
California Missions	Monterey Peninsula	San Juan Islands
California Mountains	Mormon	Seattle
Chicago	Mt. Hood (Oregon)	Tennessee
Colorado	Nevada	Texas
Dallas	New Jersey	Utah
Delaware	New Mexico	Utah Country
Denver	New York	Vancouver U.S.A.
Florida	New York City	Vermont
Georgia	Northern California	Virginia
Hawaii	Northern California Vol. II	Volcano Mt. St. Helens
Idaho	North Carolina	Washington
Illinois	North Idaho	Washington Vol. II
Indiana	Ohio	Washington, D.C.
Kentucky	Oklahoma	Wisconsin
Las Vegas	Orange County	Wyoming
Los Angeles, 200 Years	Oregon	Yosemite National Park

Forthcoming Books

Alabama	Kauai	Oahu
Arkansas	Maine	Phoenix
Baltimore	Maui	Rhode Island
Connecticut	Mississippi	Rocky Mountains
Detroit	New England	South Carolina
The Great Lakes	New Hampshire	South Dakota
Houston	North Dakota	West Virginia
Kansas		

Large Format, Hardbound Books

Beautiful America	Beauty of Washington	Lewis & Clark Country
Beauty of California	Glory of Nature's Form	Western Impressions
Beauty of Oregon	Volcanoes of the West	